Metal Clay
Beyond the Basics

Carol A. Babineau

Printed in the United States of America

12 11 10 09 08 1 2 3 4 5

Please follow appropriate health and safety measures when working with torches, kilns, and enamels. Some general guidelines are presented in this book, but always read and follow manufacturers' instructions.

Publisher's Cataloging-In-Publication Data (Prepared by The Donohue Group, Inc.)
Babineau, Carol A.
  Metal clay : beyond the basics / Carol A. Babineau.
    p. : ill. ; cm.
ISBN: 978-0-87116-250-2
1. Precious metal clay. 2. Jewelry making. 3. Beads–Design and construction. I. Title.
TT212 .B33 2008
739.27

Contents •

FOREWORD/HOW TO USE THIS BOOK   **4**

CHAPTER 1 ● EARRINGS   **5**
Silver Pod Earrings   **6**
Layered Triangle Earrings   **9**
Enameled Earrings   **11**
Textured Earrings with Peridot   **14**
Metal Clay and Ceramic Earrings   **17**

CHAPTER 2 ● BRACELETS   **21**
Textured Segments Bracelet   **22**
Sliding Bangle   **25**
Framed Beads Bracelet   **28**
Chinese Knot Bracelet   **31**
Enameled Triangles Bracelet   **34**

CHAPTER 3 ● PENDANTS   **38**
Molded Tree Pendant   **39**
Pyramid Dangles Pendant   **41**
Hollow Chrysalis with Leaf and Branch   **45**
Openwork Box Pendant   **49**
Spinning Bezel Pendant   **52**

CHAPTER 4 ● PINS   **57**
Textured Copper Insert Pin   **58**
Flowing Rings Pin/Pendant   **61**
Monet Lily Pad Pin   **64**
Metal Clay and Ceramic Name Tag   **67**
Seed Bead Vessel Pin   **71**

CHAPTER 5 ● TOGGLES & CLASPS   **74**
Lentil-shape Toggle   **75**
Leaf-and-branch Toggle with Ladybug   **77**
Double-strand Clasp   **80**
Button and T-clasp   **83**

BASICS   **86**
A repair   89
Resources   94
About the author   95

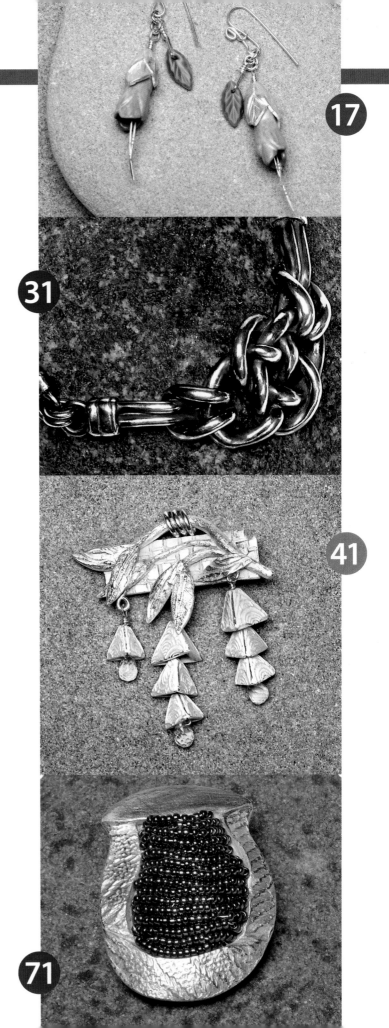

17

31

41

71

Foreword

Throughout my years of teaching and sharing what I know about metal clay, I've observed that many people long to develop their abilities to a level of excellence they know is within themselves – but they need a guiding hand. That's where this book comes in. Since I can't have each of you in my studio classroom, this book of 24 new projects is my way of coaching you. With this book at your side, I hope you will fine-tune skills, learn new techniques, and stretch your imagination.

I always challenge my students to go for the best they can do, and then I encourage them to stretch just a little bit more – perhaps even a bit beyond their comfort level. I try to do the same in my own work. That's why this book is called Metal Clay Beyond the Basics. *I challenged myself as I developed these projects. I hope you'll enjoy stretching and growing as you try them yourself!*

– Carol A. Babineau

How to use this book

Are you ready for an adventure in metal clay that takes you from the basics to beyond? That's the journey I'm ready to take with you as you create all of the (dare I say it?) outstanding jewelry designs featured in this book.

This book is organized into five chapters: Earrings, Bracelets, Pendants, Pins, and Toggles & Clasps. As you move through each chapter, the projects increase in difficulty.

If you're just starting out with metal clay, please take a look at my review of the basics (see p. 86). Here you'll find information on tools you'll need and techniques that are helpful to know. I'll confess right now: I'm a tool junkie, and my tool and supply lists can run long. Rather than repeat these items for each project, I group them as kits that are outlined in this section for your reference.

Also in this section, you'll find a review of metal clay and information on equipment for firing, finishing,

wireworking, soldering, and pickling. Because I love combining metal clay with other media, you'll also find brief introductions to working with ceramics and enamels here.

All of the projects call for some type of Art Clay product – usually my clay of choice, Art Clay 650 Slow Dry Low Fire. This relatively new formula gives you a longer working time (about 10–20 minutes, even in low humidity), can be fired as low as 1200°F (650°C), has a shrinkage rate of 8–9%, and is used with the low-fire formula of syringe clay and paste. If you like working with a different type of clay, that's fine – just take into account its shrinkage rate and be sure to fire it using the manufacturer's recommendations for time and temperature.

The firing times and temperatures given for each project assume that you are using a programmable electric kiln. Some of the smaller pieces, such as the earrings, will have other firing options, but as you progress through the book,

a larger kiln is your best option. If you don't yet have your own, check out classes or stores in your area that may offer firing services or access to a kiln.

Please read through the entire project before starting work – this goes a long way toward enjoying the creative process. As you move through the projects in this book, I think you'll be quite pleased with the range of skills you develop and the techniques you learn – not just in metal clay, but in wireworking and design as well.

I recommend that beginners start work with the first project in each chapter. After you have success with these easier pieces, you'll have the confidence to move on to the intermediate and advanced projects that follow.

Each chapter closes with a high-level jewelry project. I hope these advanced pieces will inspire you to continue where the book leaves off. Perhaps the next challenge will be designing your own metal clay jewelry!

Chapter 1
EARRINGS

Simple ideas can evolve into the most delightful pair of earrings! The projects in this chapter go beyond basic technique to show you how to transform inspiration into a piece of metal clay jewelry.

Silver Pod Earrings

TECHNIQUES
Metal clay, wireworking

Start with breakfast cereal and metal clay paste to build these graceful earrings. The metal clay technique is easy; the wirework, a bit more challenging. The white color of the unburnished pods contrasts well with the shiny silver wire.

MATERIALS

- Art Clay 650 paste: 10g
- sterling silver jump rings:
  - 18-gauge: 4 4.5mm, 4 4mm, 4 3.5mm, 4 3mm
  - 4 22-gauge, 2.5mm
  - 4 16-gauge, 3.5mm
  (all sizes inside diameter [ID])
- sterling silver wire, round, half-hard:
  - 20-gauge, 18 in. (45.7cm)
  - 24-gauge, 8 in. (20.3cm)
- 2 sterling silver head pins: 26-gauge, 1½ in. (38mm)
- a few size 15º seed beads
- 2 15mm shell beads
- 4 round cereal pieces (Kix)

TOOLS & EQUIPMENT

- 4 toothpicks
- craft foam
- film canister or similar round object

Metal clay tool kit (p. 87)

Kiln and kiln tools (p. 88)

Wireworking tools (p. 91)

Metal clay pods

Place a cereal piece on one end of a toothpick. Use a paintbrush to apply a layer of paste, leaving an opening around the base of the pod where the toothpick is inserted. Place the other end of the toothpick into craft foam to hold the piece while the paste dries **[a]**. Repeat to coat a total of four cereal pieces. Add 10–12 coats of paste to each pod, allowing the paste to dry between coats **[b]**.

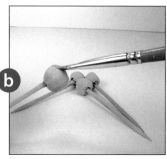

Allow the pods to air-dry for at least 24 hours. (Option: Dry in a dehydrator for 3–4 hours.) The pieces must be completely dry when they're put in the kiln or the remaining moisture could cause them to crack or explode during firing. Remove the pods from the toothpicks and place them with the holes facing up on fiber blanket **[c]**.

Fire at 800°F (430°C) for 15 minutes. During this firing segment, the cereal will turn into ash. Ramp up the kiln to 1200°F (650°C) for another 15 minutes. Remove the pods from the kiln, but do not polish them.

Wire pod stems

Drill a hole to fit 20-gauge wire in each pod directly across from the toothpick hole **[d]**. Cut two 2-in. (51mm) and two 2½-in. (63mm) pieces of 20-gauge wire for the stems. With roundnose pliers, make a small loop on one end of each wire **[e]** and check to be sure the loop fits into the toothpick hole **[f]**. Form each wire over a small container to get a graceful curve **[g]** and set aside.

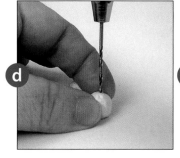

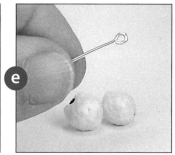

Wire pod paddles

Cut the 24-gauge wire into eight 1-in. (25.5mm) pieces. Hammer one end of each piece of wire to make a paddle **[h]**. Smooth the paddle ends with a sanding pad or an emery board. Slip one or two seed beads onto each piece of wire. With roundnose pliers,

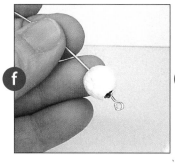

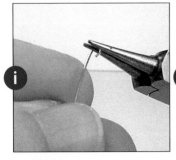

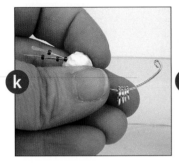

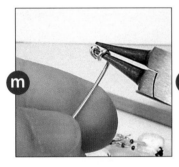

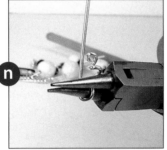

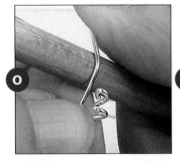

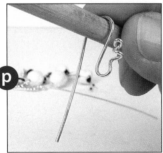

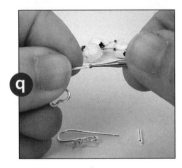

make a small loop on the non-paddle ends of the wire pieces **[i]**. Open each loop as though opening a jump ring and slip two of the loops onto the loop of a curved pod stem. Close. Repeat to add two paddle wires to each of the three remaining stems, then place one pod on each stem.

Close all the jump rings **[j]**. Place one each of the 4.5, 4, 3.5, 3, and 2.5mm jump rings on a pod stem in a graduated sequence, starting with the largest jump ring and ending with the smallest at the top. Complete the stem with a loop **[k]**. Repeat to add jump rings to the three remaining pod stems.

Insert the head pins into the shell beads and make a wrapped loop on each. Open a 3.5mm 16-gauge jump ring and add a wrapped shell bead, a short and a long flower stem, and another jump ring for hanging **[l]**. Close the jump ring. Repeat to make a second unit. These units will attach to the ear wire.

Assembly

Cut a 3-in. (76mm) piece of 20-gauge wire and make a small expanded coil about ¼ in. (6mm) long (about three wraps) around your long roundnose pliers **[m]**. Grip the wire at the base of the coil and wrap it around the lower jaw and up **[n]**.

Hold the wire between your finger and thumb of your nondominant hand with the coil facing you, and place it on the wood dowel. Wrap the wire away from you about ½ in. (13mm) from your thumb **[o]**. Continue wrapping away and down to create the large curve of the ear wire **[p]**. Add the stem/bead/jump ring units to the ear wire. Open the small coil at the top of the spiral and wrap it around the front of the ear wire to secure it. The effect will be like a tendril, which will carry out the organic design of these earrings.

Repeat the ear wire assembly steps to make a second earring, then cut the ends of the ear wires to the same length. Smooth or file the ends with sandpaper, an emery board, or a cup bur **[q]**.

Layered Triangle Earrings

TECHNIQUES
Metal clay, wireworking, keum-boo

These earrings play up the contrast of textured, sparkling silver against the richness and warmth of gold keum-boo.

MATERIALS
- Art Clay 650 Slow Dry Low Fire: 10g
- Art Clay 650 paste
- 24K gold foil
- sterling silver wire, round, half-hard: 20-gauge, 3 in. (76mm)
- one pair of sterling silver ear backs
- texturing materials (sewing trim, antique button)

TOOLS & EQUIPMENT
- triangle-shaped clay cutter: 7/16 in. (11mm) (optional)

Metal clay tool kit (p. 87)
Kiln and kiln tools (p. 88)
Wireworking tools (p. 91)
Keum-boo setup: hot plate, brass plate with hole, agate burnisher, pin

PATTERN
Trace or photocopy at 100%

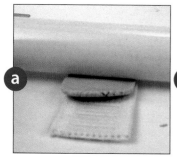

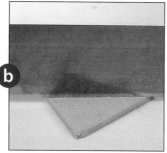

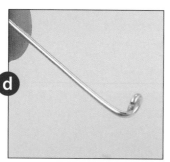

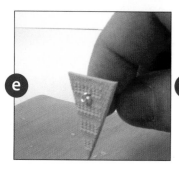

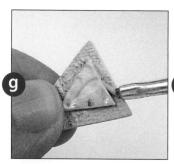

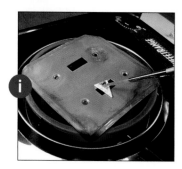

Metal clay triangles

Roll 10g of clay to 1mm thick for the base of the earrings. Texture with your desired pattern **[a]**. Using the pattern as a guide, cut two large triangle shapes with a blade **[b]** and set aside. Create a hole with a pin tool or toothpick for the earring post **[c]**.

Roll the remaining clay to 1mm thick and apply another texture. I find it interesting to apply a different pattern to this piece. Punch or cut a smaller pair of triangles following the pattern. Set aside.

Cut a 1-in. (25.5mm) piece of wire and make a small loop at one end. Bend the loop sideways to create a pad **[d]**. Place the wire inside the hole, with the pad against the textured side of the large triangle **[e]**. Add paste to the pad **[f]**, then paste the small triangle on top of the larger one, securing the wire pad. Gently press the parts together, squeezing the excess paste without distorting the small triangle. Add paste to fill and smooth any gaps **[g]**. Add paste to the back of the earring to fill in the hole. Repeat for the other earring. Fill in any cracks or dings with paste and set aside to dry completely. File and sand with progressively finer grits of sanding pads and papers.

Fire at 1290°F (700°C) for 15 minutes. Remove from the kiln. Pickle the earrings **[h]**, then place into neutralizing solution (see p. 91) until you no longer see bubbles.

Keum-boo highlights

Place the brass plate on the hot plate and turn the hot plate to high (700°–800°F/370°–430°C), which usually works best for keum-boo. Cut a piece of foil to the size of the small triangle and place it on top of the earring's small triangle. Place the earring on the brass plate with the post projecting into a hole. When the piece is hot enough, the foil will stick easily to the silver when touched with the tip of the agate burnisher. Burnish to adhere the gold to the silver, smoothing all edges **[i]**. Prick any air bubbles with a pin to release the air and burnish again. Remove from heat and allow to cool. Brush with a wire brush, polish, and burnish if desired.

TIP *For keum-boo, I use a brass light-switch plate that I shaped to fit over the heating element. The holes in the plate are handy when you have protrusions, like these earring posts.*

Trim the wire posts to 5/8 in. (16mm) and smooth the ends with a cup bur or a metal file. Add sterling silver ear backs.

Enameled Earrings

There is nothing more pleasing than adding color to silver! To make these earrings, you'll create a design with a button and learn how to use glass enamel powders.

TECHNIQUES
Metal clay, enameling, wireworking

MATERIALS

- Art Clay 650 Slow Dry Low Fire: 10g
- Art Clay 650 paste
- Art Clay 650 syringe
- sterling silver jump rings:
  - 4 16-gauge, 3.5mm ID
  - 2 22-gauge, 2.5mm ID
- sterling silver wire, round, half-hard: 20-gauge, 6 in. (15.2cm)
- Thompson 80-mesh enamel: #2340 Glass (transparent)

TOOLS & EQUIPMENT

- round cutter:
  ¾-in. (19mm) diameter
- button or stamp for molding:
  ⅝-in. (16mm) diameter

Metal clay tool kit (p. 87)
Kiln and kiln tools (p. 88)
Wireworking tools (p. 91)
Enameling tools (p. 93)

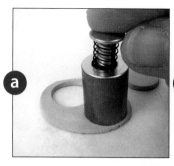

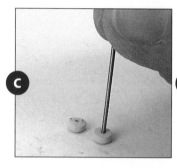

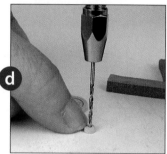

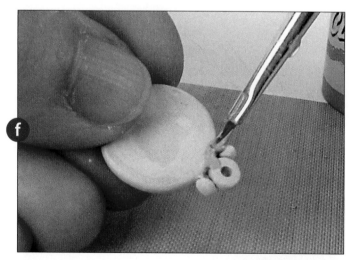

Metal clay circles

Roll 10g of clay to 2mm thick. Cut two circles with a ¾-in. (19mm) diameter cutter **[a]**. Place the button or stamp onto each clay circle and rock it gently in a clockwise motion to get a good imprint **[b]**.

Roll about half the excess clay to 1.5mm thick. Use a drinking straw to cut two small disks. Make a shallow pilot hole in each disk with a pin tool **[c].** Let all four shapes dry completely.

Roll the remaining clay into a small ball with your fingers. Using a craft knife, cut the ball into quarters and then eighths. Roll the resulting pieces into tiny balls about ⅛ in. (3mm) diameter for decoration at the top of the earrings. You will end up with a few extras. Set the balls aside to dry completely.

Use a 1.5mm bit to drill a hole in the center of the small disks you made earlier **[d]**. Sand the disks smooth. When the larger earring disks are completely dry, use a sanding pad to smooth and round the edges **[e]**. (The small disks will be added to the top of the large disks as a hanging loop for the earrings.)

Moisten the areas where the disks will be adhered, apply a small amount of syringe clay, and attach the disks. Add a small ball on each side of the disk. Smooth the backs with paste and clean up any extra paste on the sides **[f]**, then set aside to dry completely. When dry, file edges and any rough areas to a fine finish with graduated sanding papers, taking care you do not knock off the little tops. Fire at 1290°F (700°C) for 15 minutes. Cool. Brush with a stainless steel or soft brass brush and soapy water, then tumble polish or burnish until shiny.

Enamel highlights

Set the kiln temperature to hold at 1560°F (850°C) for 30 minutes. Assemble your enameling equipment (see p. 93). I recommend using a magnifying device and a bright light – it helps to see very clearly for enameling. Prepare two cups of water, one for waste water and one for clean water.

Place your clean and tumbled pieces on a piece of white paper and prepare your enamel. Wearing a face mask, place two or three tiny scoops of enamel into a

TIP

It's OK to tumble-polish the earrings after enameling with the same setup you use for metal clay: a rotary tumbler with stainless steel shot, burnishing solution, and water.

teaspoon and add a few drops of water with a pipette. Gently agitate the enamel, letting the fines rise, and pour the water off into the waste cup. Do this several times until the water in the teaspoon is clear.

Add a drop or two of Klyr-Fire to the clarified enamel. With a fine-tip paintbrush, place some of the enamel on the impressed design of the silver **[g]**. Continue until the area is covered. You may have to add water to the piece to help spread the enamel; tap each earring gently on the side to level the enamel.

Place the earrings on a mica sheet and set them on top of the kiln to dry. When dry, brush off stray grains and patch bare or thin spots. Allow the pieces to dry on top of the kiln, and recheck for stray enamel. Using a kiln fork, place the pieces into the kiln on a trivet supported by a firing rack or kiln shelf. Fire for 1½ minutes. Remove and set aside to cool.

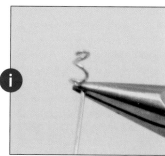

If you have a thin spot and want to add more enamel, follow the same steps: Apply, let it dry, and refire. Use an alundum stone under running water to remove excess enamel (see p. 93) and let the piece dry. Return it to the kiln to fire between 1400°F–1500°F (760°C–815°C) for 1–2 minutes. Tumble polish or burnish by hand.

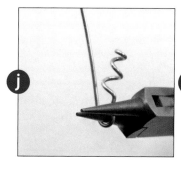

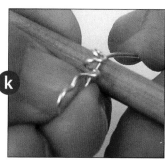

Wirework and assembly

Cut two 3-in. (76mm) pieces of 20-gauge wire and set one aside. Using roundnose pliers, make a loop at the end of one wire and wrap two more times to make a continuous loose coil **[h]**. With the coil facing you, place the long chainnose pliers directly under the coil and bend the uncoiled end of the wire 90 degrees to point down **[i]**. With roundnose pliers, grasp the wire (still facing you) and wrap away and up **[j]**. Holding the ear wire tightly in your nondominant hand, wrap the uncoiled end over a ¼-in. (6mm) diameter dowel **[k]**. Repeat with the second piece of wire to make another ear wire. Cut the ends of the ear wires to the same length and smooth with a cup bur **[l]** or file.

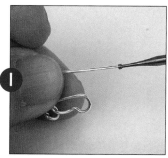

> **TIP**
> *Klyr-Fire is an enamel adhesive. It helps your enamel stay put!*

Attach a 3.5mm jump ring to the enameled disk. Attach a second 3.5mm ring to the first and then to the ear wire. Connect the coil to the ear wire with a 2.5mm jump ring. Repeat to finish the second earring.

> **TIP**
> *Enamels do not always show their true colors when hot. Wait until your piece cools completely and you should have a nice, clear color.*

Textured Earrings with Peridot

This design reminds me of little birdhouses or gourds. The clay is rolled, cut, textured, and assembled into an appealing earring set with genuine peridot stones.

TECHNIQUES
Metal clay, wireworking, stone setting

MATERIALS
- Art Clay 650 Slow Dry Low Fire: 10g
- Art Clay 650 paste
- Art Clay 650 syringe, blue tip
- 2 3mm peridots
- sterling silver jump rings: 16-gauge, 2 3.5mm ID, 2 3mm ID
- sterling silver wire, round, half-hard: 20-gauge, 6 in. (15.2cm)
- gold-filled wire, round, half-hard: 26-gauge, 4 in. (10.2cm)

TOOLS & EQUIPMENT
- texturing material

Metal clay tool kit (p. 87)
Kiln and kiln tools (p. 88)
Wireworking tools (p. 91)

Metal clay panels

Photocopy or trace the pattern. Roll 5g of clay to 1mm thick in a long, narrow shape. With a craft knife, cut the clay to follow the pattern. Divide the shape in three segments as shown **[a]**. Remove the center segment and set the other pieces aside on a nonstick sheet. Cover the pieces with plastic wrap and repeat to make a second set of shapes.

Texture the center segments and place them between the side pieces. Adhere using syringe clay and smooth the cuts with a moist brush **[b]**. Trim so you have two matching panels **[c]**. You'll be able to fine-tune the shapes at the filing stage.

With a cocktail straw, poke a hole all the way through each of the panels as shown **[d]** for the gemstone holes. Set aside. When firm, carefully turn the panels over and apply paste (or syringe clay) to the joins. Turn the panels over again and allow the paste to dry completely. Continue applying paste to the backs until the seams are gone. Dry completely. File and sand the panels until smooth using progressively finer grits of sanding papers.

Place the peridot stone in the hole to check the fit **[e]**. You may need to use a file or a setting bur to shape the hole a little. You will set the stone from the back. Using a round file, gently enlarge the hole **[f]** so the stone sits level with the back of the metal clay. Taper the hole, making the opening in the back larger than the front. Place the stone into the finished hole. Repeat with the other panel.

On the back of each panel, you'll add three dots of syringe clay that will serve as prongs to hold the gemstones. Use a fine-tip paintbrush to moisten the areas where you will place the syringe dots **[g]**. Apply a round dot of syringe clay to each area **[h]**, smoothing the shape with a moist brush if necessary. Set aside to dry completely. Sand smooth any points or rough spots on the dots.

Drill a hanging hole near the top of each panel with a 1.7mm bit. Fire at 1290°F (700°C) for 30 minutes, covering the gemstones with a bit of fiber blanket. Remove from kiln and cool. Polish, tumble, and add patina as desired.

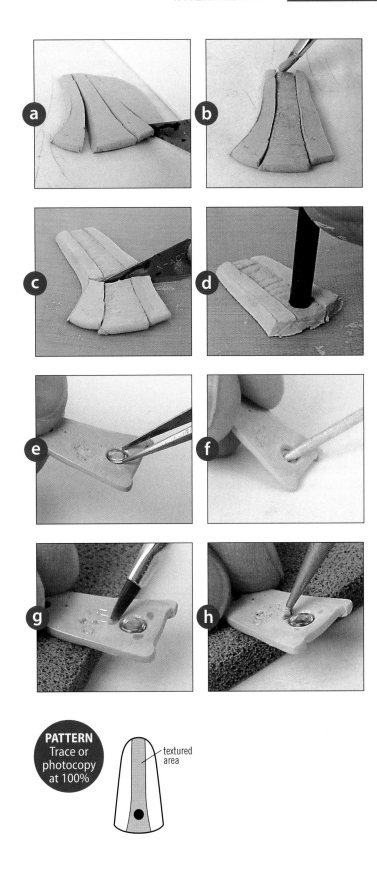

PATTERN
Trace or photocopy at 100%

textured area

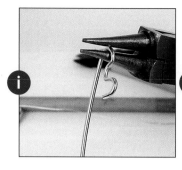

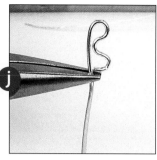

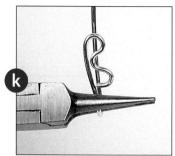

> **TIP**
> *These earrings look best with mirror-image B-shapes.*

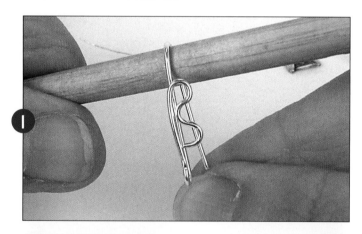

Wirework and assembly

Place one 3.5mm jump ring into each hanging hole, then add a 3mm jump ring to the first ring.

To create the ear wires, cut two 3-in. (76mm) pieces of 20-gauge wire. Do the wirework for both ear wires in one sitting for the best match, creating the first B-shape and making the second a mirror image of the first.

Using roundnose pliers, grasp the end of one wire and create a half-loop (the bottom of the B). Reposition the jaws of the pliers to make a second half-loop in the opposite direction of the first. Adjust the pliers again and make a third half-loop like the first (the top of the B) **[i]**. Continue bending the wire so that the last half-loop has a long tail pointed down alongside the curves. With chainnose pliers, grab the wire at the base of the B **[j]** and make a slight bend toward you. Place the roundnose pliers at the bend and wrap the wire end around the lower jaw and away from you so that the end points up **[k]**. Place the wire against the ¼-in. (6mm) diameter dowel about ⅛ in. (3mm) from the top of the B and wrap the wire around and down **[l]**. Create a second ear wire to mirror the shape of the first.

Cut the ends of the ear wires to the same length and smooth with a cup bur or metal file. Attach a textured panel to each ear wire.

Wrap a 2-in. (51mm) piece of gold-filled wire to bind the middle of the each B to the ear wire **[m]**. Trim and tuck in the wire ends. Repeat for the other ear wire. This is a decorative and practical finish – it ensures your earring won't slide off the ear wire.

Metal Clay and Ceramic Earrings

TECHNIQUES
Metal clay,
ceramics,
wireworking

Do you enjoy mixing your media? If so, you'll love this project. I capped rosy ceramic petals with shining silver leaves to create these fantasy flower earrings.

MATERIALS

- Art Clay 650 Slow Dry Low Fire: 10g
- Art Clay Overlay Paste
- 2 ceramic leaf beads
- low-fire earthenware clay, white, walnut-sized piece
- low-fire earthenware clay glazes: red, pink
- bead release
- sterling silver wire, round, half-hard:
  - 20-gauge, 18 in. (45.7cm)
  - 22-gauge, 5½ in. (14cm)
- sterling silver jump rings:
  - 4 18-gauge, 3mm ID
  - 2 22-gauge, 2.5mm ID
- 8 size 15º seed beads, pink

TOOLS & EQUIPMENT

- teardrop-shaped clay cutter: ½ in. (13mm) wide
- nichrome wire

Metal clay tool kit (p. 87)
Kiln and kiln tools (p. 88)
Wireworking tools (p. 91)
Ceramics tools (p. 92)

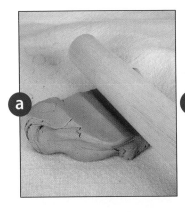

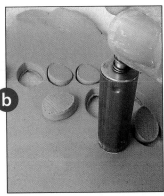

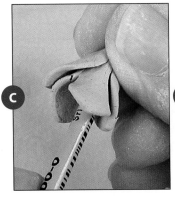

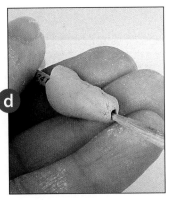

TIP
New to ceramic clay? See my introduction to working with ceramics on p. 92.

Ceramic flowers

Condition a walnut-sized piece of ceramic clay by kneading it with the heel of your hand, just as you would bread dough. Strike the clay with the wood roller to spread it and remove any air bubbles [a]. Roll the clay to 1.5mm thick. Using the brass cutter, cut eight teardrop-shaped petals (four for each flower) [b].

Curve and shape the petals with your fingers. Apply them, one at a time, to the tip of a paintbrush handle as shown, pinching the ends together where they meet [c]. Smooth the edges and any imperfections with a moistened finger, blending the petals together into the flower shape. Use a needle tool or wood skewer to poke a hole where the points converge [d]. Create two flowers and set them aside to dry for two to three days, depending on the humidity (see Tip).

When the clay is completely dry, file the edges. Wear a face mask! Ceramic dust is very fine and can be a health hazard. Place the pieces in a cold kiln and bisque-fire to 1923°F (1050°C). Allow the kiln to cool naturally; do not open the door or crash cool.

After the flowers are bisque-fired and cooled, apply two coats of pink glaze [e] and then red (or as desired), letting each coat dry before applying the next.

If you glaze the insides as well as the outsides of the flowers, position them upright with two pieces of nichrome high-fire wire dipped in bead release, then place the wires into a piece of fire brick or tall kiln posts packed with some fiber [f]. Glaze-fire to 1823°F (995°C) and let the kiln cool naturally.

TIP
Ceramic clay will dry differently in different climates. Thick work will take 3–7 days to dry completely. Most small pieces will take 2–3 days. In cold climates, clay will need at least 3 days to dry.

Check your clay pieces after 3 days by placing them in a zip-top bag; after about 20 minutes, if any moisture appears on the inside of the bag, the pieces need to dry a few more days. If your work is not completely dry, it may crack or explode in the kiln.

Metal clay caps

Roll 5g of metal clay to 1.5mm thick. Punch four teardrop shapes as you did for the ceramic pieces. Working quickly, form the leaves into a cap on one of the glazed flowers. Use a sharp pin tool or craft knife to create some leaf-like veins **[g]**. Make a hole large enough for 22-gauge wire to pass through at the base where the leaves meet. Repeat to make a second cap. Leave the clay caps in place over the glazed flowers and set aside to dry.

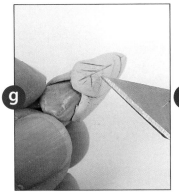
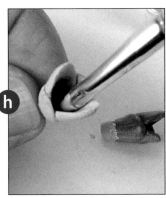

When the caps are firm, gently loosen them from the glazed flowers. When the caps move freely, place them back on the glazed flowers and dry the pieces in the dehydrator.

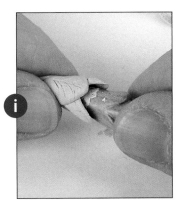

Apply overlay paste to the base of the glazed flowers and to the inside of the metal clay caps **[h]**. Place the flowers back into the caps, leaving a little "wiggle room" between the cap and flower – the caps will shrink 8–9% **[i]**. (Not allowing for this shrinkage could cause the ceramic flowers to break during firing.) Align the openings in the base of the flowers and the caps.

Position the flowers on nichrome wire and fire at 1200°F (650°C) for 30 minutes. Allow the kiln to cool to room temperature and remove the flowers from the wires. Brass brush the silver with soapy water for a matte shine. Burnish the high points and edges.

Wirework

Cut two 1½-in. (38mm) and two 1¼-in. (32mm) pieces of 22-gauge wire. Hammer one end of each wire into a paddle shape **[j]** and file the ends smooth. Place two seed beads on each wire **[k]**. Arrange the wires in two pairs – each with a long and short wire. With roundnose pliers, make a small loop at the non-paddle end of each wire; set these dangles aside.

Cut two 3-in. (76mm) pieces of 20-gauge wire. Make a loop at one end of each piece to make a wire stem.

Connect a pair of dangles to the loop of one wire stem. Repeat with the second stem and pair of dangles **[l]**.

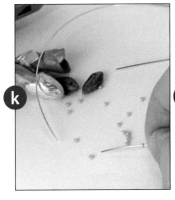
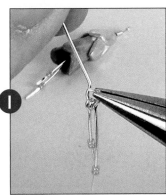

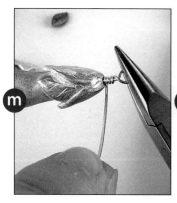

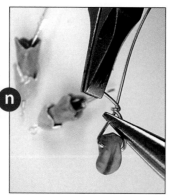

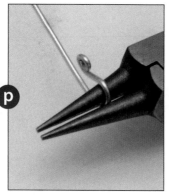

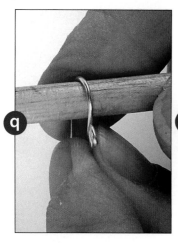

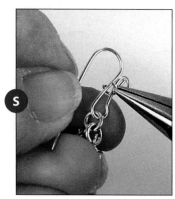

Feed a wire stem into the base of a flower and make a wrapped loop **[m]**. Repeat with the second stem and flower. Set aside.

Leaf bead wraps

In this step, you'll make a set of wraps above the leaf beads and then a wrapped loop at the top. Cut a 3-in. (76mm) piece of 22-gauge wire. Make a 30-degree bend in one wire about ¾ in. (19mm) from one end. Place a leaf bead on the long section of wire next to the bend. Make another 30° bend where the wire exits the bead so the long and short ends cross in an X above the bead. Where the wires cross, make a small bend in the long wire so it points directly upward and bend the short wire in a 45-degree angle from the long wire. Wrap the horizontal wire around the vertical wire twice **[n]** and trim the excess wrapping wire. Make a wrapped loop with the vertical wire above the set of wraps you just made. Repeat to make a second wrapped-loop leaf component.

Assembly

Cut a 3-in. piece of 20-gauge wire. With roundnose pliers, make a small curl on one end of the wire. Use your long chainnose pliers to make the curl into a small spiral **[o]**. Place the roundnose pliers about ½ in. (13mm) from the spiral, and wrap the wire under and up to make the curved base from which the earrings will hang **[p]**.

Holding the base of the ear wire in your nondominant hand, wrap the wire around a ¼-in. (6mm) diameter dowel and down **[q]**. Repeat to make a second ear wire. Trim both wires to the same length and smooth the ends with a cup bur or file.

Attach one 18-gauge jump ring to a flower loop, and add a second jump ring to the first. Add the leaf bead dangle to the second jump ring and add the second jump ring to an ear wire **[r]**. Repeat to assemble the other earring. Add a small 22-gauge jump ring or a wire wrap as shown **[s]** for security and decorative effect.

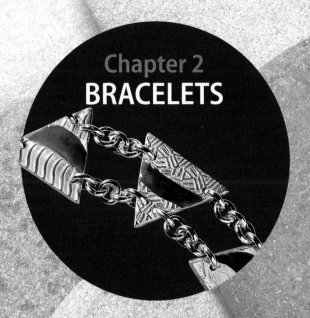

Chapter 2
BRACELETS

This chapter will take you from a basic textured bracelet to advanced enameled links. Although you may enjoy making any of the projects exactly as shown, I hope you discover the joy in tweaking shapes, sizes, and textures to create your unique versions of my bracelets.

Textured Segments Bracelet

TECHNIQUES
Metal clay,
wireworking

This project lends itself to many variations in texture.
Even the simplest texturing material results in a
fabulous bracelet!

MATERIALS
- Art Clay 650 Slow Dry Low Fire: 20g
- Art Clay 650 syringe
- Art Clay 650 paste
- 35 sterling silver jump rings:
  16-gauge, 3.5mm ID

TOOLS & EQUIPMENT
- texturing material (I used ribbon)
- bracelet mandrel (or soft-drink can)
- square clay cutter: $^7/_{16}$ in. (11mm)

Metal clay tool kit (p. 87)
Kiln and kiln tools (p. 88)
Wireworking tools (p. 91)
Pickling setup (p. 91)

Textured links

Tape a piece of nonstick material to the largest step of the bracelet mandrel **[a]**. Select or create a texture for the links. Roll 20g of clay to 1.5mm thick, place the texture on the clay, and roll. Cut the textured clay into three strips, one approximately 1¾ x ½ in. (44 x 13mm) and two 1½ x ½ in. (38 x 13mm).

Place the strips on the mandrel until firm **[b]**. Remove the links from the mandrel and stand them on their sides to dry completely.

> **TIP**
> *These measurements make a bracelet to fit an average wrist size of 6–6½ in. (15.2–16.5cm). For extra length, use more jump rings or add two ½-in. (13mm) links between the longer links.*

Toggle loop and bar

Roll the excess clay and texture it in the same way as the bracelet links. Cut a ¾ x ⅝ in. (19 x 16mm) rectangle using your straight-edge blade. Leaving a wider border on one short side, use the square cutter to cut out the center of the rectangle, creating the toggle loop component.

Roll the remaining clay into a snake and flatten to 1.5mm thick. Texture, then trim the clay to 1⅜ x ¼ in. (35 x 6.5mm) for the toggle bar **[c]**.

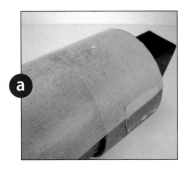

> **TIP**
> *Using the widest point on the bracelet mandrel creates gently curved links. Use a soft-drink can if you don't have a mandrel.*

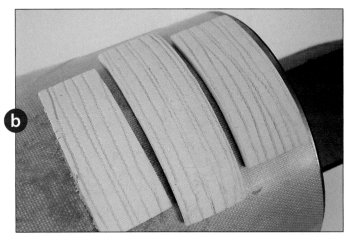

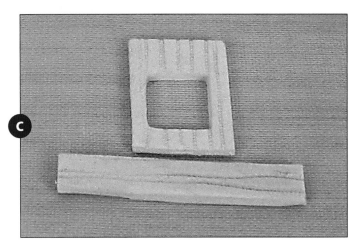

> **TIP**
> *A rule of thumb is to make the toggle bar slightly longer than the width of the opening times two. To function well, the bar needs a short lead of chain or linked jump rings.*

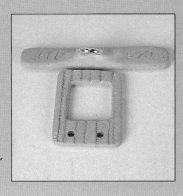

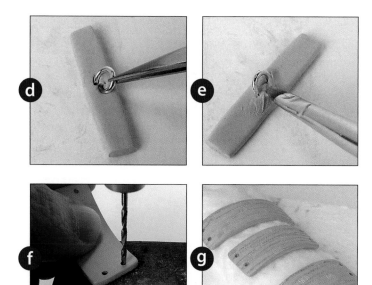

TIP *To help a toggle bar sit well on the wrist, open the jump ring slightly and position it at an angle to the bar.*

Insert a jump ring into the midpoint of the toggle bar **[d]**. Build a mound of syringe clay or paste at the base of the ring. When dry, add more syringe clay and smooth with a damp paintbrush **[e]**. Set aside until the jump ring is firmly set. You may have to add more paste or syringe clay to make a smooth join. Set the toggle components aside to dry completely.

Once dry, file and sand all the pieces to a fine finish, rounding the corners if desired. Use a progression of medium, fine, and superfine grit sanding pads, then change to polishing papers up to 8000 grit. This will give you an excellent finish: The finer the finish in the dry state, the smoother your fired product.

Using a 1.7mm drill bit and working from the back, carefully drill four holes for jump rings in each link component **[f]** and two holes in the wider border of the toggle loop component. (I place my pieces on a rubber block for good support while drilling.) Place these holes no closer to the edge than the width of the bit.

Use a piece of fiber blanket in the kiln to support the link shapes **[g]**. Fire all the components at 1290°F (700°C) for 30 minutes. Remove and cool. To remove the oxidation from the sterling silver ring, pickle and polish the toggle bar (see p. 91). Brush all pieces with a stainless steel or brass brush and hand-polish, burnish, or tumble-polish.

Assembly

Use both pairs of pliers to open 34 jump rings. Attach a jump ring to each hole in the links. Connect the links with additional jump rings **[h]**. Use jump rings to attach the toggle loop to one end. Add jump rings to the other end as shown **[i]**; connect the end link's pair of single chains to one jump ring, then add a chain of three more jump rings, attaching the last one to the toggle bar. Lengthen the bracelet if necessary by adding a few more jump rings.

Sliding Bangle

Movement in a piece always attracts my attention. I envisioned this bracelet as a small roller coaster spinning around a track, with beads separating the segments like hookups on a train. A bonus: This piece makes a delightful "cha-cha" sound on your wrist!

TECHNIQUES
Metal clay, soldering, metal working, wireworking

MATERIALS

- Art Clay 650 Slow Dry Low Fire: 20g
- 16 sterling silver jump rings: 16-gauge, 4.5mm ID
- sterling silver wire:
  - 12-gauge, half-round, dead-soft, 16–20 in. (40.6–50.8cm)
  - 20-gauge, round, half-hard, 12 in. (30.5cm)
- 8 4mm green garnet rondelles
- 4 6mm red tourmaline rondelles

TOOLS & EQUIPMENT

- texturing material (I used elastic)
- bracelet mandrel (or soft-drink can)
- square clay cutter: 1/2 in. (13mm)

Metal clay tool kit (p. 87)

Kiln and kiln tools (p. 88)

Wireworking tools (p. 91)

Soldering setup (p. 91)

Pickling setup (p. 91)

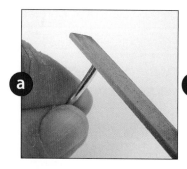

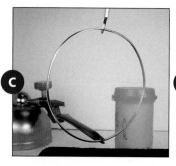

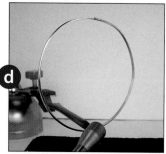

TIP

If you want to skip the soldering step, an easy alternative is to buy a pair of ready-made sterling silver bangles. If you'd like to learn more about torches and soldering, check your local technical college for beginner classes or look into some of the wonderful resources listed on p. 94.

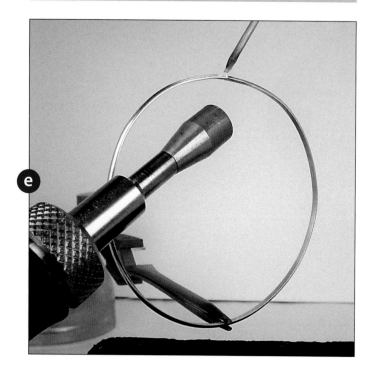

TIP

Before you begin this project, determine your size by trying on a bangle that fits, or create a test bangle from inexpensive copper wire. To create my bangle, I used an 8-in. (20.3cm) circumference (the third step on a four-step bracelet mandrel), which fits very small hands and wrists.

If you increase the bangle circumference, you'll need to make the clay sections a bit longer, add beads to the wrapped-loop connectors, or do both.

Soldered rings

Cut two pieces of 12-gauge half-round wire to your desired bangle measurement. Use a 4-cut flat hand file to smooth the ends **[a]**. Bend the wire around the mandrel by hand **[b]** or by tapping with a rawhide mallet. Check the fit and the join – you want enough tension in the wire so no gap shows where the ends meet. Hold the ring up to the light; if you see any light at the wire ends, curve the ring a bit beyond the meeting point so tension holds the ends tightly together. Repeat to shape a second ring. Clean both rings with steel wool.

Place one ring in a third hand with the join at the top and apply paste flux to the entire piece **[c]**. Place a solder pallion on the join. Using a soft, bushy flame, heat the ring evenly, starting at the bottom **[d]**. Gradually move up to the join and pass the flame back and forth from below the join to draw the solder down. It may be necessary to adjust the position of the pallion with the pick **[e]**. When the flux becomes glassy, the solder is near its melting temperature. Watch closely for the solder to flow down through the join.

Remove the flame, quench, and pickle the ring to remove oxidation and flux. Repeat for the second ring. Rinse the rings in water and dry them. Use sandpaper or a file to remove firescale and any excess solder. Polish and set aside until assembly.

Metal clay panels

Choose a texture for the bracelet panels. Tape a piece of nonstick sheet to the bracelet mandrel. Roll 20g of clay to 1.5mm thick and texture it [f]. Cut four panels from the textured clay, each 1⅜ x ¾ in. (35 x 19mm) [g]. This panel size creates a small bracelet – make these pieces longer for a medium or large bangle. Place the panels over the prepared mandrel to dry in a curved shape until firm. Remove from the mandrel and stand the panels on their sides in the dehydrator, adding support if needed, until completely dry. File the edges and add paste or syringe clay to any cracks or divots. Allow the paste to dry and sand smooth again. Use a hand drill with a 1.7mm bit to make three evenly spaced holes on each panel's short ends.

Support the curved panels on a fiber blanket and fire at 1290°F (700°C) for 30 minutes. Cool; remove from the kiln. Brush with a brass brush and soapy water.

Assembly

Gather the bangle materials: soldered rings, textured panels, rondelles, jump rings, and 20-gauge wire. Using longnose and flatnose pliers, open the jump rings. Cut four 3-in. (76mm) pieces of wire. With roundnose pliers, make the first step of a wrapped loop, slide the wire through the middle hole of one panel [h], and finish wrapping the loop. Add rondelles to the wire in a 4mm, 6mm, 4mm sequence. Make the first step of a wrapped loop on the other wire end, slide the wire through the middle hole of another panel, and finish wrapping the loop [i].

Continue linking the panels together in this way to form a circle. Your circle of linked panels should be the same diameter as the soldered rings. If not, disassemble the linked panels and repeat the first assembly step using smaller or larger beads (or fewer or more) as necessary.

To attach the linked panels to the soldered rings, slide a jump ring through a corner hole of one of the textured panels, add one soldered ring, and close the jump ring [j]. Continue connecting all the panels to the first ring in this way [k]. Repeat to connect the second soldered ring to the opposite sides of the panels [l, m]. Tumble polish.

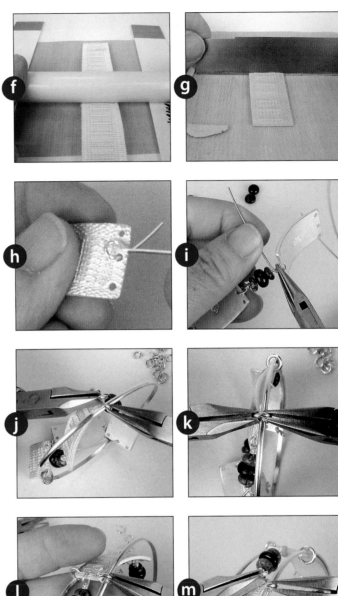
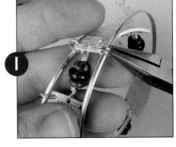
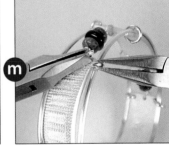

Framed Beads Bracelet

Although you could cut these frames from a single rectangle of clay, I prefer the look of joined strips. The resulting seams give the bracelet extra dimension and character.

MATERIALS

- Art Clay 650 Slow Dry Low Fire: 25g
- Art Clay 650 paste
- Art Clay 650 syringe
- sterling silver wire:
   22-gauge, round, half-hard,
   18 in. (45.7cm)
- sterling silver jump rings:
   16-gauge, 20 3.5mm ID
   15 4mm ID
- 9 8mm stone tube beads
- 9 size 11º seed beads

TOOLS & EQUIPMENT

- texturing material
   (I used wallpaper)
- bracelet mandrel (or soft-drink can)

Metal clay tool kit (p. 87)

Kiln and kiln tools (p. 88)

Finishing tools and supplies (p. 90)

Wireworking tools (p. 91)

Pickling setup (p. 91)

Metal clay frames

Tape a piece of nonstick sheet to the widest point on the mandrel **[a]**. Use about 5g of clay to roll a snake 4 in. (10.2cm) long and ⅛ in. (3mm) in diameter. Place the snake on the texture and roll to 1.5mm thick. Trim the width to ¼ in. (6mm), then cut two 1½-in. (38mm) strips and two ½-in. (13mm) strips. Place the short strips between the long strips. Using syringe clay and paste, adhere the strips to make a frame **[b]**. Place the frame over the prepared mandrel to dry in a curved shape. Repeat to make a total of four frames.

To create the square toggle frame, roll the remaining clay into a ⅛-in. diameter snake. Texture and flatten the snake to 1.5mm thick. Trim the width to ¼ in., then cut two 1-in. (25.5mm) strips and two ½-in. strips. Assemble and finish the toggle frame and place over the mandrel. Let all of the frames dry until firm; they will be fragile at this stage.

Gently remove the frames from the mandrel and add paste to the backs to smooth the seams **[c]**. Let the paste dry. Repeat the process as necessary to get a seamless surface on the back of each frame. Allow all the frames to dry completely. Sand and smooth the frames to a fine finish using progressively finer grits of sanding pads and then polishing papers. Use a scribe or other pointed tool to retexture any areas that have been obscured by paste or sanding.

To drill holes in the frames, work with the concave curve facing up. For the beaded frames, mark the positions for six ladder rung holes **[d]** as shown in the pattern, and drill holes using a 1.5mm bit. These are the holes for the wire-wrapped beads. Mark the jump ring holes at each corner as shown and drill these with a 1.7mm bit. Drill a jump ring hole in two corners of one long side of the toggle frame.

For the toggle bar, roll the excess clay into a ³⁄₁₆-in. (5mm) diameter snake, tapering one end. Trim to 1½ in. Open a 4mm jump ring slightly and place it at the midpoint of the bar **[e]**.

TIP *These measurements make a 7-in. (17.8cm) bracelet – that's end to end. It fits a small wrist like mine. For a larger wrist, add jump rings or make longer metal clay frames: 1¾ in. (44mm) for medium or 2 in. (51mm) for large.*

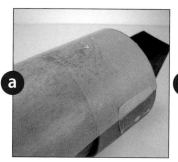
a

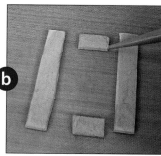
b

c

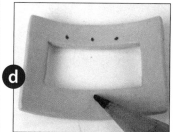
d

e

PATTERN
Trace or photocopy at 100%

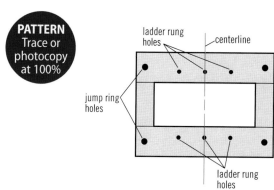

ladder rung holes

centerline

jump ring holes

ladder rung holes

TIP *Use an alternating bead pattern in each frame: seed bead, stone bead on the first wire; stone bead, seed bead on the second wire; and seed bead, stone bead on the last wire.*

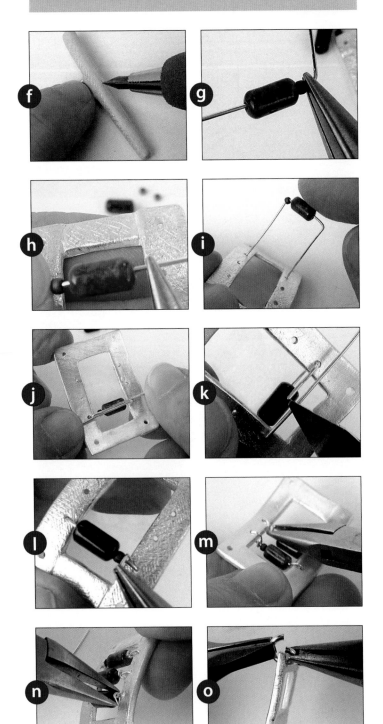

Build a mound of syringe clay at the base of the ring. Fill any holes with syringe clay or paste and smooth with a paintbrush. Set the toggle bar aside to dry completely. When dry, file, sand, and smooth. Scribe any texture that has been obscured by pasting and sanding **[f]**. Use fiber blanket to support the frames during firing. Fire the frames and the toggle bar at 1290°F (700°C) for 30 minutes. Remove and cool. Pickle the toggle bar to remove oxidation from the jump ring. Brush all the pieces with a wire brush and soapy water. Hand-polish or tumble.

Assembly

Cut nine 3-in. (76mm) pieces of 22-gauge wire. With long chainnose pliers, grasp the wire about 1 in. (25.5mm) from one end and bend the wire 90 degrees. Slip the beads on the first wire **[g]**.

Check the fit of this rung against the opening in the frame **[h]**. Use your pliers to grasp the straight end of the wire next to the bead, leaving 2mm of wire between the bead and the tips of the pliers. Bend the wire 90 degrees to make a large staple. Insert the staple into one pair of rung holes **[i]** and cross the wires against the back of the rung **[j]**. Trim the wire ends at the midpoint **[k]**. Bring one wire end to the front of the frame and wrap it once **[l]**. Trim the end, if needed, and snug the wrap. Repeat on the other side. Add the two remaining bead rungs to this frame in the same way **[m, n]**. Continue until you've added all the beaded rungs to the remaining two frames.

Open 14 4mm jump rings and slide one through each jump ring hole in each frame, including the toggle frame. Close each jump ring **[o]**. Open four 3.5mm jump rings and connect them to the 4mm jump rings between the beaded links. Close the jump rings. Open six 3.5mm jump rings. Use them to make two three-link chains. On one end of the bracelet, use the three-link chains to connect a link and the toggle frame. Open four 4mm jump rings. On the remaining end of the bracelet, attach two jump rings to each jump ring in the link. Open another 4mm jump ring. Slide it through the two end jump rings. Make a five-link chain using 3.5mm jump rings. Attach one end to the end 4mm jump ring. Attach the other end to the toggle bar. Lengthen the bracelet by adding more jump rings, if needed.

Chinese Knot Bracelet

TECHNIQUES
Metal clay, wireworking, Chinese knotting

The centerpiece of this bracelet is a Chinese double coin knot, so-named because it looks like a pair of overlapping antique Chinese coins. Practice tying the knots with cord so you can move swiftly after you open the package of metal clay.

MATERIALS

- Art Clay 650 Slow Dry Low Fire: 45g
- Art Clay 650 paste
- Art Clay 650 syringe
- 15 sterling silver jump rings: 16-gauge, 3.5mm ID

TOOLS & EQUIPMENT

- bracelet mandrel (or soft-drink can)
- texturing material (I used ribbon yarn)

Metal clay tool kit (p. 87)

Kiln and kiln tools (p. 88)

Finishing tools and supplies (p. 90)

Wireworking tools (p. 91)

Pickling setup (p. 91)

TIP *I used a snake roller – a long acrylic sheet (see p. 87) – for this project because it produces a dense yet workable length of clay. Using a metal clay extruder or a syringe is an option.*

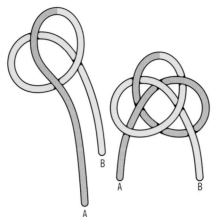

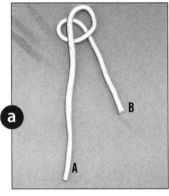

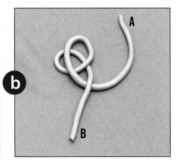

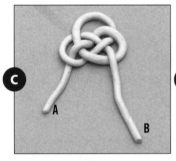

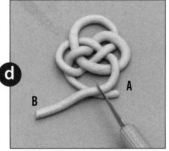

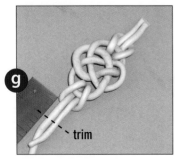

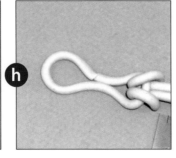

Centerpiece knot

Roll 20g of clay into a snake approximately 10 in. (25.4cm) long and ⅛ in. (3mm) in diameter. Follow the steps below to create the centerpiece knot. The illustration at left shows the two ends (A and B) in different colors to clarify the knotting sequence.

Working quickly but gently, make a loop and bring end B underneath the loop **[a]**. Bring end A under end B and up **[b]**, then through the top loop from the front, and down through the left loop **[c]**. Overlap the ends to finish the knot and trim with a craft knife **[d]**. Adjust the knot so that one pair of opposing loops allows room for the lark's head connectors. In my example, the loop where I made the cut and the loop opposite had more room and became the side loops. Paste the seam together, and add paste or syringe clay to any cracks. Shape the knot gently over the widest point on the bracelet mandrel so the side loops curve down **[e]**; allow the knot to dry until firm.

Lark's head connectors

Roll 30g of clay into six uniform 5-in. (12.7cm) snakes, all ⅛ in. (3mm) in diameter. Mist four snakes lightly with distilled water, wrap in plastic, and set aside. Make each of the two unwrapped snakes into a U-shape. Using a lark's head knot, attach one U-snake to one of the centerpiece knot's side loops. Repeat with the second U-snake and the other side loop **[f]**. Trim the ends to extend ½ in. (13mm) past the lark's head loop **[g]**. Gently turn the assembly over and adhere the ends together with paste. (Do not add paste to the curved knot.) When the paste is dry, shape the assembly gently over the bracelet mandrel and allow to dry completely.

Remove two of the reserved snakes and form each into a U-shape. Make a lark's head knot to attach the first snake to the second. Trim the straight ends of the first snake to ½ in. past the lark's head loop as above. Make a loop with the second snake and pinch the loop together, placing the join at the pinch **[h]**. Paste and smooth the join. This is the toggle loop end. Place the assembly over the mandrel to dry completely.

Remove the two remaining snakes and fold each into a U-shape. Make a lark's head knot to attach the first snake to the second. Trim the ends of the knot ½ in. past the loop **[i]**. Trim the ends of the second snake to create a ¾-in. (19mm) long loop. This end will connect to the toggle bar. On the back, adhere the ends together with paste and let dry. Place the assembly over the mandrel and allow to dry completely **[j]**.

Toggle bar

Roll a quarter-sized piece of excess clay into a ⅛-in. diameter snake, cut in half, place the halves side by side, and trim to 1¼ in. (32mm) long. Join the two snakes with paste to make the toggle bar, smooth, and let the paste dry. Open a jump ring slightly and insert at the midpoint of the bar **[k]**. Use syringe clay to adhere the ring in place and allow to dry completely.

When all the components are completely dry, smooth any cracks or fissures with paste, dry the paste, and sand until smooth.

Textured bands

Roll 10g of clay to .75mm thick, creating a long strip at least ½ in. (13mm) wide. Roll again to add texture (I used ribbon yarn) **[l]**. Trim to ⅜ in. (9mm) wide. Cut the strip into eight ¾-in. (19mm) bands. Put three aside in plastic wrap. Wrap one band around the end of each lark's head connector unit and the toggle bar connector. Place the seams on the back side of the components and leave an opening where you will seat a jump ring. Trim the seams, add paste, smooth, and dry the paste. Add syringe clay to the openings in the ends to fill them and place one jump ring in each end **[m]**. Wrap one of the reserved bands at each end of the toggle bar. Wrap the remaining band around the pinch in the toggle loop end **[n]**. Trim the seams, add paste, smooth, and dry the paste. Allow all the components to dry completely.

Firing and assembly

Support the components with fiber blanket and fire at 1290°F (700°C) for 30 minutes. Cool, remove from the kiln, pickle, and soak in a neutralizing bath (see p. 91). Brush with a wire brush and soapy water. Use double jump rings to connect the components. Add a chain of three single jump rings to the toggle bar and connect it to the toggle bar connector with double rings. Tumble polish, or use a liver of sulfur solution and polish just the high spots for an aged look.

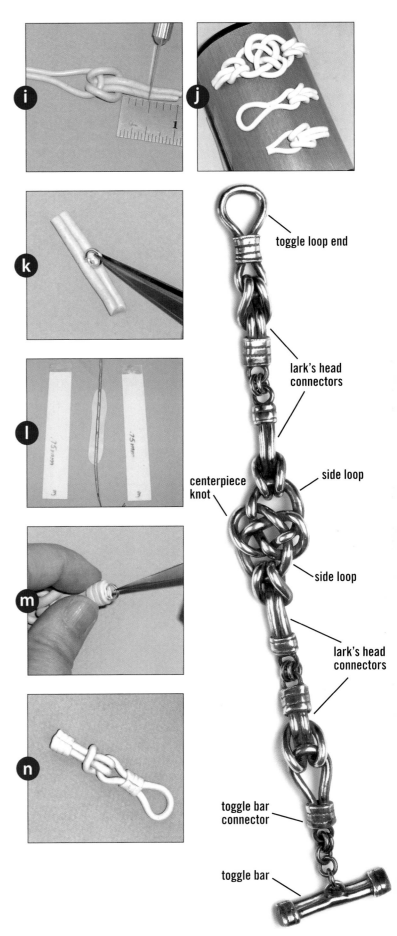

Enameled Triangles Bracelet

TECHNIQUES
Metal clay, enameling, wireworking

The idea for this bracelet came from a ribbon that had a twist in it. To make it, you'll create textured triangles, cut them apart, reattach them, and then enamel a ribbon of color across the center of each.

MATERIALS

- Art Clay 650 Slow Dry Low Fire: 40g
- Art Clay 650 paste
- Art Clay 650 syringe
- sterling silver jump rings:
  16-gauge, 44 3mm, 20 3.5mm,
  2 4mm, 2 4.5mm (all ID)
- Ninomiya leaded enamels: NG-320 (light turquoise), LT64-1 (ultramarine blue)

TOOLS & EQUIPMENT

- triangle clay cutters: 1 in. (25.5mm),
  ½ in. (13mm)
- variety of texture sheets, rubber stamps, or other texturing materials

Metal clay tool kit (p. 87)

Kiln and kiln tools (p. 88)

Finishing tools and supplies (p. 90)

Wireworking tools (p. 91)

Enameling tools (p. 93)

Triangles

You will make one triangle at a time, so keep the unused clay well-hydrated in its original package, a clay keeper, or under plastic wrap as you work.

Roll 6g of clay to 2mm thick. Place the rolled clay onto the texture and roll again to texture it **[a]**. With the large triangle cutter or a craft knife, cut a triangle. Using a craft knife **[b]**, cut two curves to divide the triangle into three parts as shown on the pattern.

Roll the center section to 1.5mm to remove the texture. Use water and/or paste to smooth the area if needed. Add syringe clay along the edges of the textured segments that will touch the smooth segment **[c]** and reassemble the three pieces into the original triangle shape **[d]**. Smooth the extra paste at the seams with a brush. Trim the triangle and reshape, if needed, with a straight-edge blade. Using a moist brush, smooth the center piece again if necessary **[e]**. Use paste or syringe clay to build up a slight edge on the sides of the smooth section to contain the enamel **[f]**.

Create five triangles this way using a different texture on each triangle. Set all aside until firm. Make sure the triangles are securely bonded, then turn them over and apply paste to the backs to create the look of one seamless piece **[g]**. Continue to add thin layers of paste, setting the pieces aside to dry between layers, until the backs are perfectly smooth and uniformly thick. Sand the pieces, add paste to any visible seams, dry, and sand again until smooth.

Line up the triangles with the back sides facing up. Use a pencil to mark placement for the jump ring holes. The marks should line up across all the triangles **[h]**. Place each triangle on a small rubber block and drill holes using a 1.7mm drill bit **[i]**.

> **TIP**
> *The pattern shows all the jump ring holes in the top and bottom segments so the center enameled sections will not have holes.*

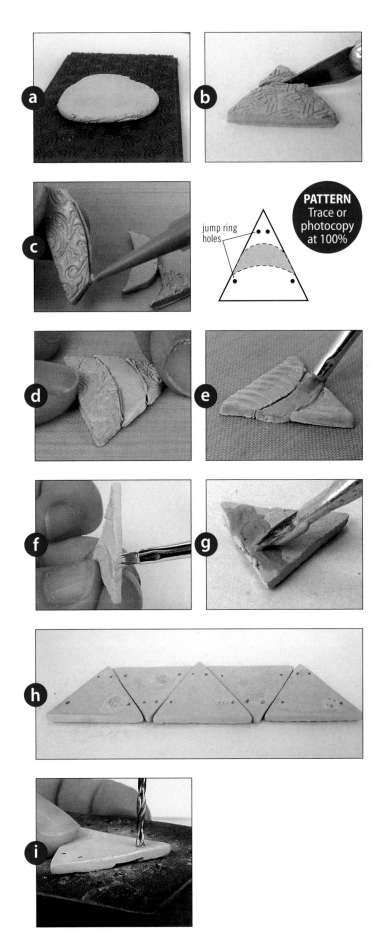

PATTERN
Trace or photocopy at 100%

jump ring holes

TIP

If you don't have enameling experience, take a few minutes to review the basics of enameling tools and techniques on p. 93.

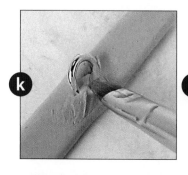

TIP

By grouping the triangles on a sheet of mica, you can fire more than one at a time.

TIP

Take extra precautions when working with leaded enamels. Always wear a face mask while working with the granules, and wash your hands and work surface with water thoroughly afterward.

Toggle and bar

Roll 10g of clay to 1.5mm thick and add texture. Cut a 1-in. triangle for the toggle and use the small triangle cutter or a craft knife to cut out the center of the toggle. Using a straight-edge blade, trim an angled bar about 1⅜ in. (35mm) long from the textured clay **[j]**. Set the triangle aside to dry completely while you work with the toggle bar.

When the bar is firm, make a small syringe clay mound in the center back. Place a slightly open 4mm jump ring in the mound, angling the ring slightly, and smooth with a moist paintbrush **[k]**. Add more paste or syringe clay if necessary to smooth. Set aside to dry completely. Sand and finely finish the toggle and bar.

When all the triangle and toggle pieces are completely dry, fire at 1290°F (700°C) for 30 minutes. Because the bar includes sterling silver, pickle the bar, then place it in a neutralizing solution until it stops bubbling (see p. 91). Remove. Brush all pieces with a wire brush, then tumble polish. Dry in the dehydrator to remove any remaining moisture.

Enameling the triangles

Preheat the kiln to 1550°F (845°C). Each time you open the kiln door, a heat loss occurs, so it's better to set it slightly higher than needed. For enameling, you want the temperature in the 1400°F (700°C)+ range.

Clarify the enamels as you did for the Enameled Earrings (see p. 12). Place a small amount of the light turquoise in a plastic spoon and add a few drops of distilled water. Add some Klyr-Fire enamel adhesive. Scoop up some enamel with a fine-tip paintbrush and place it into the smooth center segment of the triangle. Continue until the area is filled. You may need to add a drop or two of water with a pipette to the metal clay triangle to help unload the enamel from the brush. A needle tool also can be helpful in applying enamel.

Add enough water with your pipette to smooth out the enamel and then tap the edge of the piece with a heavy metal tool handle to settle the grains. Use the ultramarine blue enamel to add depth **[l]** and to create color variations as desired.

Fill in all of the segments, level the enamel, then place the triangles on top of the kiln to dry.

When the enamel is dry (it will look powdery), clean the triangles under a magnifying glass with a fine-tip brush or pick. Move or remove enamel grains as necessary. Any stray grains left after firing will need to be ground away with an alundum stone, so it's easier to take care of them at this point. Place the triangles on a sheet of mica supported by a trivet, and place the trivet on a kiln shelf.

Wearing protective lenses and using a kiln fork, place the kiln shelf with trivet carefully into the kiln onto kiln posts **[m]** and close the door. After two minutes, open the door to see if the enamel is glossy. If it is, remove the shelf from the kiln and place it on a fire-proof surface to cool. If not, close the door and allow the temperature to return to at least 1400°F (760°C). Fire for one more minute and check again. When the enamel reaches the glossy stage, remove the shelf and allow the triangles to air cool. Finish with a wire brush. Polish.

Assembly

Open 20 3.5mm jump rings. Slide one through a hole in a triangle and close the jump ring. Repeat to attach a 3.5mm jump ring to each hole in each triangle.

Open a 3mm jump ring, scoop up two closed 3mm jump rings, and close the ring. Repeat to make 12 three-link chains.

Arrange the triangles so the tips alternately point up and down. Attach an end link of a three-link chain

to each 3.5mm jump ring. On each end of the bracelet, attach a 3mm jump ring to the end of one of the three-link chains, making it a four-link chain.

Make a four-link chain using 3mm jump rings. On one end of the bracelet, attach one end of the four-link chain to both the four- and three-link chains. Attach the other end to the toggle bar **[n]**.

On the other end of the bracelet, attach a 4mm jump ring to both the four- and three-link chains. Attach a 3mm jump ring to the 4mm jump ring. Attach a second 3mm jump ring to the 3mm jump ring. Attach two 4.5mm jump rings to the loop half of the clasp and to the last 3mm jump ring **[o]**.

Chapter 3
PENDANTS

Since you can create just about anything you can imagine with metal clay, there's no reason to limit yourself to the same old style of flat pendant. This chapter presents designs ranging from hollow forms to an incredible spinning bezel pendant.

Molded Tree Pendant

TECHNIQUES
Mold making with polymer clay, sculpting metal clay

The base of this piece is a mold made from simple and readily available materials: polymer clay, a small bead box, and a wood dowel. You can use it over and over if you like. I think of the tree trunk, branches, and roots as sculpture – have fun "growing" your own tree!

MATERIALS

- Art Clay 650 Slow Dry Low Fire: 15g
- Art Clay 650 paste
- Art Clay 650 syringe: green tip, blue tip
- polymer clay, 1 oz. (about ¹/₂ a package)
- cornstarch

TOOLS & MATERIALS

- polymer clay (pasta) machine* (optional)
- plastic bead box top, 1¹/₄ in. (32mm) square
- toaster oven*
- wood dowel, ⁷/₁₆ in. (11mm)
- texturing material
- drinking straw

Metal clay tool kit (p. 87)

Kiln and kiln tools (p. 88)

Finishing tools and supplies (p. 90)

*Dedicated to nonfood use

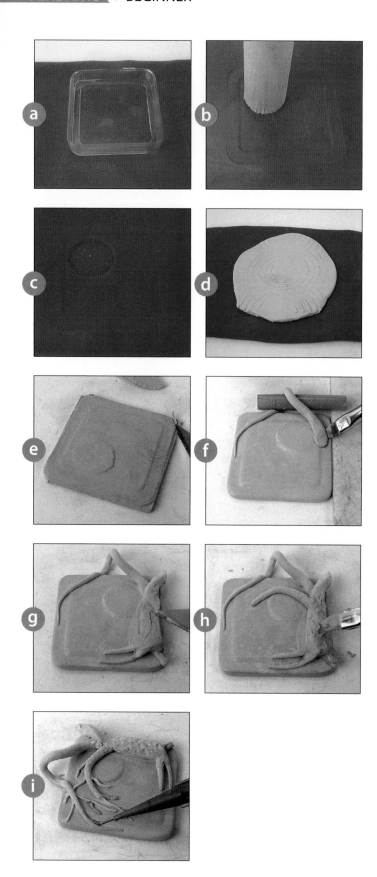

Polymer clay mold

Condition about ½ package of polymer clay by kneading or rolling through the pasta machine. Using the machine or an acrylic roller, roll to ¼ in. (6mm) thick. Lightly dust the top of the plastic box with cornstarch and press it into the polymer clay to make a crisp impression **[a]**. Press the end of the wood dowel into the upper left corner **[b]** to create a deep full-moon impression within the square **[c]**. Bake the mold in a toaster oven according to the instructions on the polymer clay package. Set aside to cool.

Metal clay pendant

Lightly oil the mold. Roll 10g of metal clay to 2.25mm thick and to the approximate area of the mold. Place the clay in the mold, making sure it reaches all four corners. Texture the clay in the mold **[d]**. (The textured side will be the back of the pendant.) Carefully remove the clay from the mold and repair any cracks or fissures. Trim the edges, round the corners **[e]**, and set the panel aside to dry.

Roll half the remaining metal clay into a snake about ⅛ in. (3mm) in diameter. Taper one end to a fine point; measure from this end to about 1½ in. (38mm) and cut to create the largest branch, which is the pendant's bail. Form the branch around a piece of drinking straw and use paste to adhere the ends to the panel **[f]**. Set any remaining rolled clay aside under plastic to use for other branches and roots.

Roll the remaining metal clay to a snake about ¼ in. (6mm) diameter for the tree trunk. Cut to about ⅞ in. (22mm) long and adhere to the base with paste. Score the trunk with a craft knife for texture **[g]** and apply paste in small dabs to create the look of bark **[h]**.

Apply more branches as desired, using any remaining snakes and syringe clay. Use the green tip first, then apply finer branches with the blue tip **[i]**. Set aside to dry completely. Fill unwanted cracks, dry, and sand well, leaving some bark texture. Fire at 1290°F (700°C) for 15 minutes; cool. Brush with a wire brush and soapy water. Tumble polish if desired. Use a liver of sulfur solution to add depth and color if desired.

Pyramid Dangles Pendant

TECHNIQUES
Metal clay, wireworking

This pendant reminds me of a flowering wisteria vine. The pyramid dangles add gentle movement to the piece.

MATERIALS

- Art Clay 650 Slow Dry Low Fire: 30g
- Art Clay 650 paste
- Art Clay 650 syringe: green tip, blue tip
- fine silver wire: 20-gauge, 3 in. (76mm)
- sterling silver wire: 22-gauge, 12 in. (30.5cm)
- 3 sterling silver jump rings: 16-gauge, 4.5mm ID
- 3 top-drilled 6mm briolettes
- 8 size 8º triangle seed beads

TOOLS & EQUIPMENT

- triangle clay cutters: ⁷/₁₆ in. (11mm), ³/₈ in. (9mm)
- texture sheets (I used patterns of bricks and crescents)

Metal clay tool kit (p. 87)
Kiln and kiln tools (p. 88)
Finishing tools and supplies (p. 90)
Wireworking tools (p. 91)

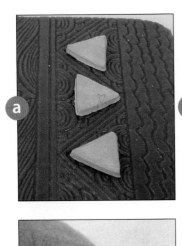

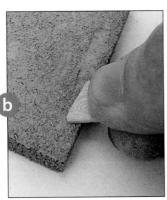

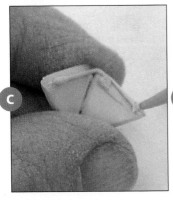

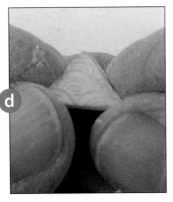

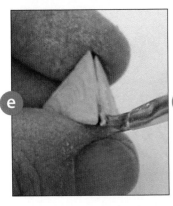

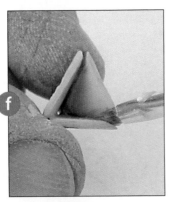

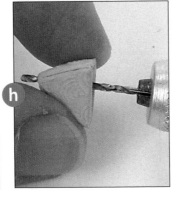

Pyramids

Roll 10g of clay to 1mm thick. Punch out nine large and twelve small triangles.

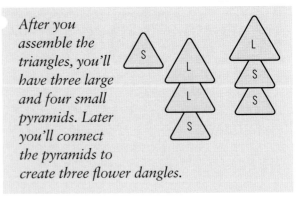

After you assemble the triangles, you'll have three large and four small pyramids. Later you'll connect the pyramids to create three flower dangles.

Texture all of the triangles (I used a crescent pattern) **[a]**. Set aside all of the triangles to dry completely. Once dry, file or sand a beveled edge on two sides of every triangle **[b]**. (After the triangles are made into pyramids and are completely dry, you'll sand the bottoms smooth.)

Moisten the beveled edges of the large triangles. Using a syringe with a green tip, place a line of syringe clay along each edge **[c]**. Gently assemble the triangles to create a pyramid **[d]**. Repeat to assemble all the remaining triangles into pyramids.

Sand smooth and add paste or syringe clay to any gaps or uneven sections. Moisten along the seams and again apply a thin line of syringe clay to fill any gaps between the pieces. Smooth the excess clay with a damp paintbrush **[e]**. Smooth the extra syringe clay on the inside as well, taking care not to fill the very top of the pyramid where the wire will be inserted **[f]**.

Place all the pyramids aside to dry completely. Add paste or syringe clay to any cracks or gaps. Dry. Sand and file, making the bottom flat and even. Using a syringe with a blue tip, make a decorative line down each seam of every pyramid **[g]**. Allow the syringe clay to dry completely and sand gently. Carefully drill a hole at the top of each pyramid with a 1.3mm drill bit to create a clean opening **[h]**.

Base, branches, and leaves

Roll 10g clay to 1.5mm thick. Apply a brick texture (or texture of your choice), trim the clay to 1¼ x ½ in. (32 x 13mm), and set aside.

Roll 5g of clay into a 2mm-diameter snake to be used for three branches. Position the top branch on the base and trim with a craft knife. This branch will become the bail. Add two more branch shapes, trim, and use paste or syringe clay to adhere them onto the base, smoothing as you go **[i]**.

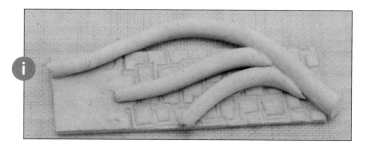

Make three 1-in. (25.5mm) eye hooks from the fine silver wire. Insert them into the base as shown **[j]**, adding syringe clay or paste as needed.

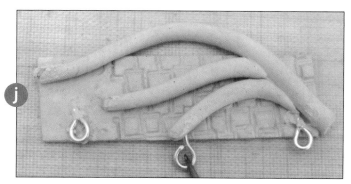

Roll 5g of clay to 1mm thick. Using a craft knife, cut six small, thin leaf shapes and scribe the veins **[k]**. Use paste and syringe clay to adhere onto the branch tips as desired, taking care to hide the base of each eye hook. Shape the leaves as desired and prop with toothpicks or wood skewers **[l]**.

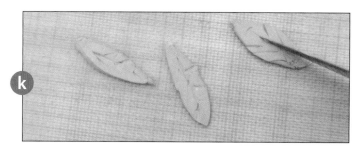

Apply extra paste to the branches to simulate a bark texture **[m]**. Smooth any paste or syringe clay that adheres the leaves and branches and allow all to dry completely. Sand or file smooth any irregularities, the edges of the base, and the back.

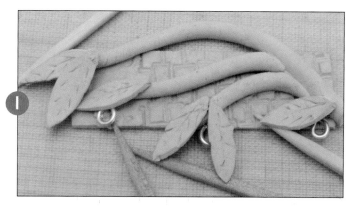

Fire at 1290°F (700°C) for 15 minutes. Remove from the kiln; cool. Polish with a wire brush and soapy water. Use 3M radial disks on a rotary tool to get into the corners and crevices. Burnish the high points on the leaves.

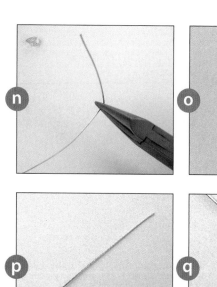

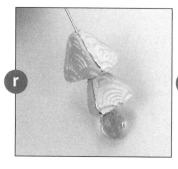

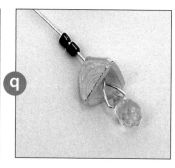

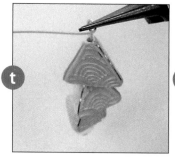

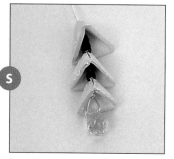

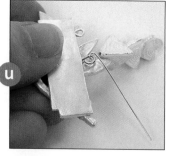

Assembly

Cut a 2-in. (51mm) piece of sterling silver wire and bend it about 1½ in. (38mm) from one end **[n]**. Add a briolette to the long end of the wire and bend the long end of the wire up. Cross the wires and wrap the shorter wire around the long one **[o]**. Trim and tuck the short wire end, leaving the long end **[p]**.

Add one small pyramid to the wire, then add two triangle beads **[q]**. These beads will separate the pyramids and allow for movement. Add a large pyramid **[r]**, two triangle beads, and another large pyramid **[s]**.

Create the first part of a wrapped loop **[t]**. Place the pyramid assembly onto the center eye hook **[u]**, finish wrapping the loop, and tuck in the wire end **[v]**.

Repeat the assembly pattern for the right eye hook, but add two small and then one large pyramid, following the pattern on p. 42.

For the left eye hook, use a briolette and one small pyramid. Add the three jump rings to the bail branch to attach to the chain of your choice.

Hollow Chrysalis with Leaf and Branch

I've experimented with many unusual armatures for shaping hollow beads. This project uses two flax pills. They're flexible and they make perfect oval forms for the chrysalis. And they're good for your heart!

TECHNIQUES
Metal clay, hollow forms

MATERIALS
- Art Clay 650 Slow Dry Low Fire: 15g
- Art Clay 650 paste
- Art Clay 650 syringe
- sterling silver wire:
  14-gauge, round, half-hard,
  3 in. (76mm)
- 2 flax pills (or other oval armatures)
- small natural leaf

TOOLS & EQUIPMENT
- drinking straw for branch/bail
- oval cutter: 7/8 in. (22mm)
- round cutter: 1/2 in. (13mm)
- texture sheet (I used wallpaper)
- carving tool (optional)
- needle tool or small brass hole cutter

Metal clay tool kit (p. 87)

Kiln and kiln tools (p. 88)

Finishing tools and supplies (p. 90)

Soldering setup (p. 91)

Wireworking tools (p. 91)

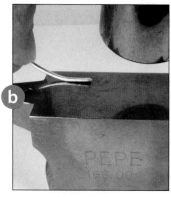
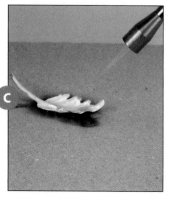

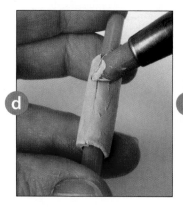

Leaf and stem

Apply a thin layer of paste to the back of the leaf and allow to dry completely. Continue to add layers of paste, letting it dry between layers, until the paste is approximately 1mm thick or weighs at least 2g **[a]**.

Cut a 1-in. (25.5mm) piece of sterling silver wire and lightly hammer one end to flatten it. Curve the wire to simulate a leaf stem **[b]**.

Attach the flattened wire end to the leaf, using syringe clay in a line on either side of the leaf's main vein. Brush paste onto the lines to smooth them. Allow the paste to dry, then add more paste if necessary to smooth the piece. Set aside to dry until firm.

Sand any rough edges smooth. When the piece is completely dry, torch fire **[c]** for 1½ minutes outdoors or with adequate ventilation (see Tip). Allow to cool. Set aside for assembly.

Bail tube

Roll 5g of clay to 1mm thick. Shape the clay over a drinking straw to make a 1-in. long tube. Seal and smooth the seam **[d]** and place the tube in the dehydrator to dry. Remove the tube from the straw and add paste or syringe clay to smooth both the inside and the outside seams. Set aside to dry.

Use paste to create a rough texture resembling bark on the tube **[e]**. If desired, use a knife to add carved lines before adding the paste texture.

Dry completely. Sand or file any rough edges. Sand the ends of the tube by moving them over a sanding pad.

TIP
*Torch-fire the leaf **only** if you have a ventilation system that will exhaust the burnoff. An alternative is to kiln-fire at 400°F (200°C) for 10 minutes.*

Hollow chrysalis

Oil the pills that will be the armatures for the chrysalis. Roll 10g of clay to 1.5mm thick. Use the oval cutter to cut out two ovals from the clay, one for each half of the chrysalis. Gently work one piece of clay over each flax pill until it is halfway around, taking care not to stretch it too thin **[f]**. Roll the clay-covered armatures on the texture **[g]**. Set these pieces aside to air dry.

> **TIP**
> *For the texture on the chrysalis, I used a small piece of wallpaper with a pattern of very organic, wavy lines.*

When the pieces are dry, remove the "shells" by pinching the pills lightly until the metal clay pops off. Sand the edges of the shells so they will adhere evenly to each other **[h]**. Hold the shells together and use a round file to gradually make a hole **[i]**. Make the opening large enough to accommodate the 14-gauge wire of the stem.

Cut about 1½ in. (38mm) of the wire and make a loop at one end. With chainnose pliers, grasp the neck of the loop and bend the wire 90 degrees. Apply syringe clay around the edge of one of the chrysalis halves, skipping the hole, and place the wire into the chrysalis half **[j]**. Join the two halves. Smooth the outer seam. Add syringe clay or paste as needed to fill any gaps **[k]** and set aside to dry until firm. If desired, use a carving tool to add additional lines and texture.

Roll the excess clay to 1mm thick. Punch out a ½-in. (13mm) diameter disk and use a needle tool or tiny brass cutter to make a hole in the center **[l]**. Slip the disk onto the wire **[m]**. Using paste, mold the disk to the chrysalis, smoothing it and securing the bond between the wire and the chrysalis. This cap will help secure the wire stem coming out of the top of the chrysalis. (You'll trim the wire later when you attach it to the branch.)

Using a very fine (.7mm) bit in a hand drill, make a vent hole in the bottom of the chrysalis. Set the piece aside to dry completely.

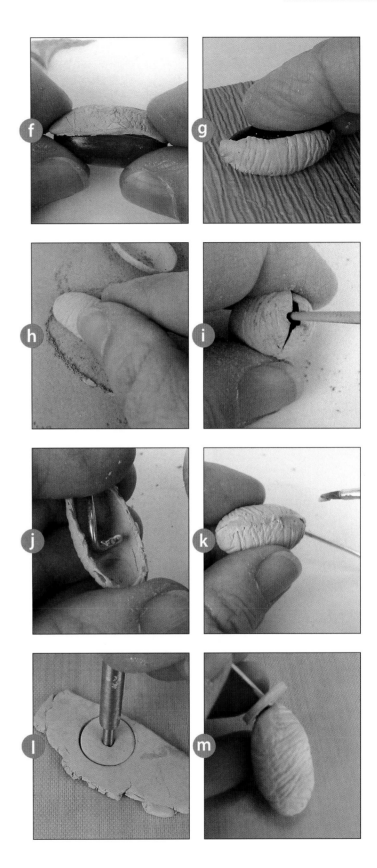

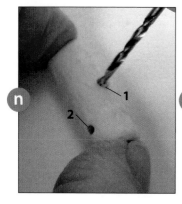

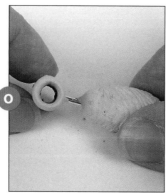

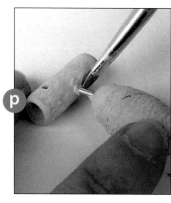

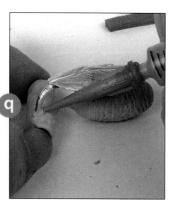

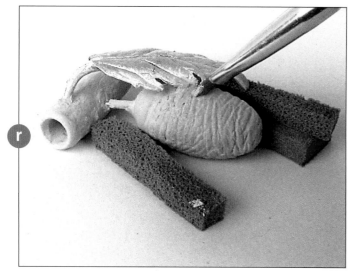

Assembly

Drill two holes in the bail tube with a large (1.5 or 2mm) bit as shown **[n]**. (Hole #1 will hold the wire connecting to the chrysalis and hole #2 will hold the leaf stem.)

Test-fit the pieces and trim any excess wire, making sure the wire doesn't protrude into the bail tube **[o]**. Add syringe clay to hole #1 in the bail tube and embed the chrysalis wire into it. Smooth and add more paste or syringe clay as needed **[p]**, covering the entire wire. Support the piece with fiber blanket to hold its shape while it dries.

Insert the fired leaf stem into hole #2 and add syringe clay around the stem **[q]**. Smooth with a brush. Add some syringe clay to the back of the leaf where it touches the chrysalis. Press the leaf and chrysalis together lightly and smooth any excess paste. Prop the assembly so it does not sag **[r]**.

Dry completely, then file or sand off any irregularities. Use fiber blanket to prop the piece in the kiln. Fire at 1290°F (700°C) for 30 minutes. Remove from the kiln and brush the leaf to a shine. Burnish the leaf and the high points of the branch, leaving the chrysalis white.

Openwork Box Pendant

This piece uses only metal clay and a jump ring, but the construction is challenging. You'll insert rolled clay into a frame, then join the frame on all four sides to create a clever, see-through box.

MATERIALS

- Art Clay 650 Slow Dry Low Fire: 20g
- Art Clay 650 paste
- Art Clay 650 syringe
- sterling silver jump ring:
    16-gauge, 4.5mm ID

TOOLS & EQUIPMENT

Metal clay tool kit (p. 87)

Kiln and kiln tools (p. 88)

Finishing tools and supplies (p. 90)

Pickling setup (p. 91)

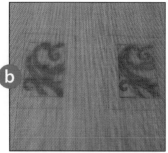
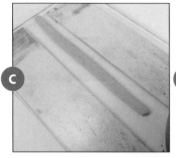

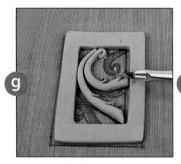

PATTERN
Trace or photocopy at 100%

Openwork panels

Trace or photocopy the pattern **[a]**, and tape a piece of nonstick sheet over it **[b]**. Use this work surface as a guide to gauge the size of the frames and apply the inner design.

Roll 10g of clay into a ⅛-in. (3mm) diameter snake and flatten to 1.5mm thick **[c]**. Trim to ⅙ in. (4mm) wide and cut the strip into four pieces to make a frame as shown in the pattern. Add syringe clay where the strip ends meet and push together. Smooth the excess syringe clay with a brush **[d]**. (The back of the frames will be filled and finished later.) Set aside to dry completely. Repeat to make the second frame in the same way. Place both frames in the dehydrator to dry completely.

Carefully fill any gaps at the joins with paste or syringe clay, let dry, and file smooth. Gently hold the two frames together and sand until smooth **[e]**. Use care, because these pieces are fragile. Place the frames on the pattern work surface, smooth side up.

Roll a dime-sized piece of clay (about 3g) into a snake, tapering one end to a point. Position the snake in one frame, using a paintbrush to shape it to follow the curve shown on the pattern. Using a craft knife, make two shallow cuts in the snake and pull the points out a bit with the tip of the knife **[f]**. Repeat to create the second curved shape **[g]**. Don't adhere these pieces to the frame yet. Set them aside to dry.

Using excess clay, roll two more narrow snakes and lay them on the template; coil, shape, and trim as needed. Allow all the pieces to dry completely.

Sand the small parts to remove rough edges. Add syringe clay or paste to the ends that touch the frame **[h]** and adhere. Repeat to add curved shapes to the second frame.

When the openwork panels are firm, turn them over and add paste or syringe clay to the back, creating a smooth surface. Take care to avoid getting any syringe clay on the front of the piece. Let dry, and carefully sand the two openwork panels smooth with progressively finer sanding papers. Repair any cracks or breaks, let dry, and sand again.

Frame walls

Roll the remaining clay (about 7g) into a 1.5mm-thick sheet at least 1 x 1¼ in. (25.5 x 32mm). Texture the sheet if desired and cut the clay into strips: two ¼ x 1¼ in. (6.5 x 32mm) and two ¼ x ⅞ in. (6.5 x 22mm).

Apply syringe along one edge and the two ends of one long textured strip [i]. Adhere the strip, textured side out, to the back of an openwork panel. Support the assembly as it dries with a sanding pad cut to fit [j]. Repeat to attach the other long strip and one short strip to the panel. When firm, add more syringe clay if necessary to fill any gaps [k]. Cut a 2mm gap in the center of the remaining textured strip and attach it to the back panel.

Roll a pea-sized piece of excess clay into a ⅛-in. diameter snake. Cut four ⅜-in. (9mm) lengths and adhere one to each corner with syringe clay to add support [l].

Add a small support platform of clay under the gap [m]. Insert a jump ring into the gap [n]. Add syringe clay to fill and smooth with a brush [o]. Set aside until firm.

Apply syringe clay along the edges of the textured strips [p] and attach the second openwork panel [q]. Smooth any excess paste, fill gaps, and set aside to dry. Fill any new gaps that occur. Sand smooth and prop the box with fiber blanket [r]. Fire at 1200°F (650°C) for 30 minutes. Pickle the piece to remove oxidation from the sterling silver jump ring. Brush with a wire brush and soapy water, then tumble polish. Enhance the design, if desired, with a liver of sulfur solution, and polish again.

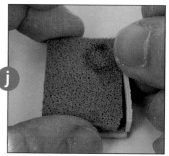

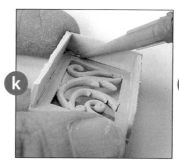
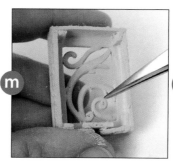

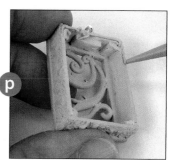

Spinning Bezel Pendant

A friend and talented gem cutter created the square, stepped cut of this fantastic nine-carat amethyst. If your gemstone isn't square and you're up for a challenge, adapt the instructions to fit the shape and size of your stone.

MATERIALS

- Art Clay 650 Slow Dry Low Fire: 55g
- Art Clay 650 paste
- Art Clay 650 syringe: blue tip, green tip
- 14mm square cabochon
- sterling silver wire:
  - 16-gauge, round, half-hard, 2 in. (51mm)
  - 20-gauge, round, half-hard, 4 in. (10.2cm)
- sterling silver jump ring: 16-gauge, 4.5mm ID
- sterling silver tubing: 10-gauge, 2.56mm OD, 1.93mm ID, 1 in. (25.5mm)

TOOLS & EQUIPMENT

- texture sheets in two patterns
- jeweler's saw and 2/0 blade (or mini tube cutter)
- rotary tool and stone-setting burs: 1mm, 2mm

Metal clay tool kit (p. 87)

Kiln and kiln tools (p. 88)

Finishing tools and supplies (p. 90)

Wireworking tools (p. 91)

Pickling setup (p. 91)

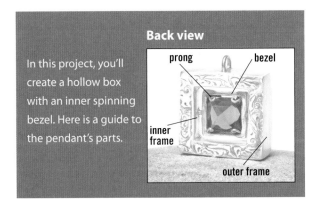

Back view

In this project, you'll create a hollow box with an inner spinning bezel. Here is a guide to the pendant's parts.

prong   bezel

inner frame

outer frame

Bezel

Roll 10g of clay to 1.5mm thick. Cut two ¾ x ³⁄₁₆ in. (19 x 5mm) and two ⅝ x ³⁄₁₆ in. (16 x 5mm) strips. Using a small brass circle cutter or a cocktail straw, punch out two holes in the center of each of the shorter strips **[a]**, using the pattern as a guide. Add syringe clay along the ends of the two shorter strips and attach the longer strips to make the bezel walls **[b]**. (You can also do this in two stages, making two L brackets and joining them with syringe clay.) Allow the bezel to dry completely, using a piece of sanding pad cut to size as an armature. Insert the 16-gauge wire to check the hole alignment; remove. Add more paste or syringe clay to the corners if needed **[c]**. Allow to dry completely. Gently sand the bezel, gradually smoothing the surfaces **[d]**. Slightly bevel the top and bottom edges by holding the piece at an angle while sanding **[e]**. Use care at this point because the bezel is fragile.

Roll a dime-sized piece of clay (about 3g) into a 1.5mm-diameter snake and cut in half. You will reinforce the sides of the bezel and add detail by wrapping a snake along each side, temporarily covering the holes. Add paste along one side of the bezel and attach a snake. The ends should wrap around the top and bottom corner, extending about ⅛ in. (3mm). With a craft knife, trim and taper the top and bottom ends of the snake **[f]**. Smooth with a moist paintbrush. Use the blunt end of the brush to flatten the snake where it covers the hole **[g]**. (You'll re-drill the hole later.) Repeat to apply the other snake to the other side.

Roll a 1mm-diameter snake (about 2g); apply it all the way around the perimeter of the bezel front **[h]** and smooth the join with paste. Cut four 1-in. (25.5mm) pieces of 20-gauge wire, make a loop at one end of each wire **[i]**, and trim the straight ends

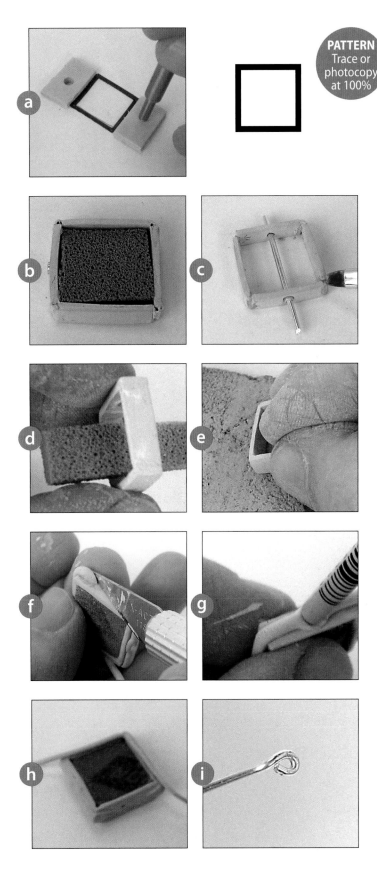

PATTERN Trace or photocopy at 100%

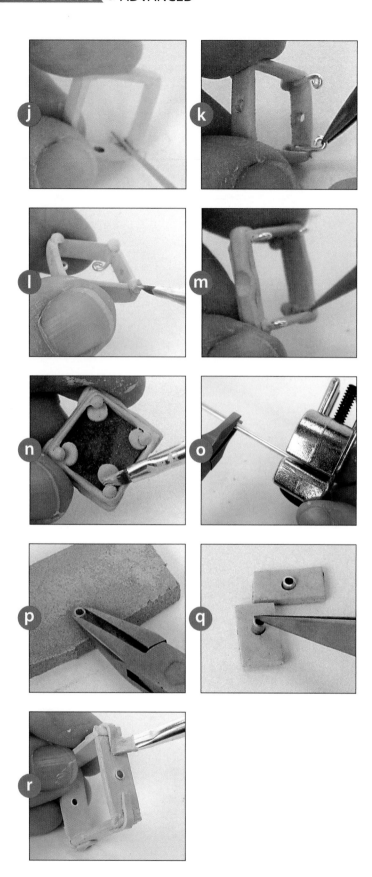

(not including the loops) to ¼ in. (6mm). These loops will become the prongs that hold the back of the stone. Use a round file to make a shallow channel along each inside corner of the bezel to hold the wires **[j]**. Handle the bezel gently – it's very fragile.

Apply a line of syringe clay along each channel and place a wire prong in each corner, smoothing as you go **[k]**. (See the back view on p. 56 for orientation of the prong loops.) Roll a tiny amount of clay into four small balls. Place one ball at each corner of the bezel front using syringe clay. Add some watered-down paste to these corner supports to help smooth them **[l]**. Use the blue syringe tip to reinforce the wire prongs **[m]**. Make four more balls and flatten them. Adhere these under each corner ball, using the sanding pad as support **[n]**. Apply paste or syringe clay to any gaps and allow to dry completely.

Inner frame

Use a jeweler's saw with a 2/0 blade (or a mini tube cutter) to cut two ⅛-in. (3mm) pieces of 10-gauge tubing **[o]**. Sand both ends of the tubes smooth **[p]**.

Roll a quarter-sized piece of clay (about 5g) to 1.5mm thick. Cut two strips to ⁵⁄₁₆ x ¾ in. (8 x 24mm) and two slightly shorter, ⁵⁄₁₆ x ¹⁵⁄₁₆ (8 x 19mm). Using a small brass cutter or cocktail straw, punch a hole in the middle of the two short strips. Insert the tubes in the wet clay **[q]** and allow all the strips to dry completely. Add syringe clay along the ends of two short strips and attach the long strips to make a square inner frame. Smooth and add paste if needed to the joins. Add thin bands of clay to each corner of the inner frame for reinforcement **[r]**. Allow the inner frame to

> **TIP**
> *If your cabochon is a different size than mine, your bezel will need to be a different size as well. Use these calculations to arrive at a size that allows for shrinkage. These figures assume a shrinkage rate of 9%; if the type of metal clay you're using has a different rate, factor that in.*
> *100 minus shrinkage rate (9%) = 91*
> *100 divided by 91 = 1.10*
> *cab size x 1.10 = bezel size needed*

dry completely and add more paste or syringe clay if needed. Gently sand the square, gradually smoothing the inner surfaces. Test-fit the bezel; it should fit inside the inner frame.

Outer frame back and sides

Roll 10g of clay to 1.5mm thick and texture it. Place the inner frame on top of the clay and use a craft knife to cut out the inner square of clay from the textured sheet. Trim around the outside of the inner frame, leaving about a ³⁄₁₆ in. (5mm) clay border **[s]**. This is the back of the outer frame. Place a line of syringe clay around the inner edge of the outer frame **[t]**. Adhere the inner frame to the outer frame. Add paste to any visible cracks or gaps. Allow the assembly to dry completely and sand smooth.

Use a 1.7mm drill bit to re-drill the holes in the bezel sides. Insert the 16-gauge wire through one hole of the inner frame, through the bezel, and out the other side of the bezel and the inner frame. Trim the wire so it extends just 1mm past the tube ends on each side. Add syringe clay to the wire where it enters the bezel to secure the wire to the bezel **[u]**.

Roll 10g of clay to 1.5mm thick for the side walls of the outer frame. Using the back of the outer frame as your guide, cut four pieces, two slightly shorter as before. Join the two long sides and one short side with syringe clay or paste, and smooth with a moist brush **[v, w]**.

Cut the remaining short side to leave a 2mm gap at the midpoint where the jump ring will be attached. Adhere with paste or syringe clay to complete the side walls. Reinforce the gap by moistening with a brush **[x]** and then applying a small strip of clay underneath (between the outer and inner frame). Allow the assembly to dry completely. Apply syringe clay to the gap, place a jump ring into it **[y]**, and smooth. Place the foam sanding pad back into the bezel from the back to support the assembly as it dries.

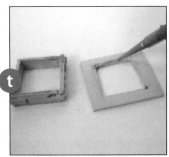

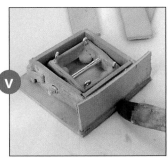

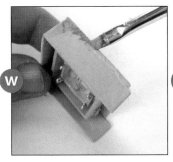

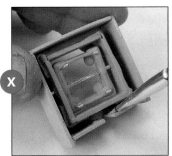

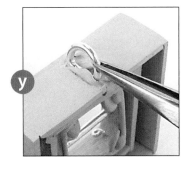

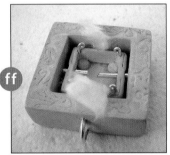

Outer frame front

Roll 15g of clay to 1.5mm thick and texture it. (I like to use different textures on the front and the back.) Cut the textured clay into a strip approximately ¼ in. (6mm) wide to fit on top of the inner and outer walls of the frame. Place the strip on the front of the frame and use a craft knife to trim at a 45-degree angle at each corner **[aa]**. Allow the clay to firm up slightly and test-fit the pieces to see if additional trimming is needed **[bb]**.

Run lines of syringe clay along the edges of the inner and outer frames and attach the textured strips **[cc]**. Add syringe clay to the mitered corners **[dd]**, smoothing as needed **[ee]**. Allow the assembly to dry completely. Sand and finish, and remove the foam support. Prop fiber blanket under and around the bezel **[ff]**. Carefully cut the bezel-spinning wire in half to allow the clay to shrink evenly as it fires. Fire at 1290°F (700°C) for 30 minutes. Remove from kiln and cool. I prefer not to pickle this piece because it is hollow; remove any oxidation from the jump ring with sandpaper.

Finishing and stone setting

Trim the wire inside the bezel so it is flush with the inner wall. File if necessary. Apply liver of sulfur sparingly to the inside of the bezel and the outer faces of the pendant; allow to darken. Hand-polish and burnish the high points.

Place the stone in the bezel with the prongs at the back. If the inner bezel walls need refining, use a rotary tool and a stone-setting bur to grind out small amounts of silver from the corners until the stone slips in. Use a bezel pusher or burnisher to bend the prongs toward the stone to hold it securely **[gg]**. The bezeled stone should spin freely within the frame.

Back view

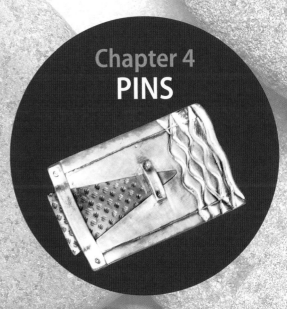

Chapter 4
PINS

I never tire of exploring different ways to make pins that combine metal clay with other media. Whether you want to incorporate beads, ceramic, enamel, or mixed metals, this chapter offers plenty of inspiration.

Textured Copper Insert Pin

This pin features an exciting mix of metals and texture. It's more than just a rectangle of clay – it also has a frame for extra dimension.

TECHNIQUES
Metal clay, metal working

MATERIALS

- Art Clay 650 Slow Dry Low Fire: 20g
- Art Clay 650 paste
- Art Clay 650 syringe
- fine silver screw-type pin finding
- copper sheet:
  20-gauge, $1^1/_2$ x 1 in. (38 x 25.5mm)
- copper cleaner
- two-part epoxy

TOOLS & EQUIPMENT

- rolling mill with brass texture plate (or planishing hammer and metal stamps)
- metal shears (or jeweler's saw and bench pin)
- bench vise
- texture rolling tool

Metal clay tool kit (p. 87)

Kiln and kiln tools (p. 88)

Finishing tools and supplies (p. 90)

Wireworking tools (p. 91)

Pickling setup (p. 91)

Copper triangle

Texture the copper sheet in a rolling mill **[a]**. Use any type of texture you like – I used a brass texture plate. Use metal shears or a jeweler's saw to cut a triangle from the copper 1⅜ in. (35mm) long by ⅝ in. (16mm) at the base. Place the triangle in a bench vise and file the edges smooth **[b]**. Finish smoothing the edges with sandpaper. If desired, clean the triangle with copper cleaner, then wash with soap and water and dry. Set aside.

Metal clay rectangle

Roll 20g of clay to 1.5mm thick. Cut to 1 x 1⅝ in. (25.5 x 41mm). Lightly press the copper triangle into the left side of the rectangle **[c]**; the base of the triangle should extend beyond the left edge of the rectangle about ⅛ in. (3mm). Use a texture roller to add interest to the right side of the rectangle **[d]**.

Remove the copper triangle and turn the clay rectangle over. With the pin stem and hinge screwed in place, press each of the threaded bolts of the pin finding into the clay to make small divots on the rectangle back **[e]**. Remove the bolts and set aside. Paste any cracks or dings in the rectangle and allow to dry completely. File the back smooth.

With the excess clay, roll a ⅛-in. diameter snake and flatten to 2mm. Trim the edges with a straight-edge blade **[f]**. Place the strip alongside the metal clay rectangle and cut two long and two short strips to frame the rectangle. Moisten the edges of the rectangle, add syringe clay along the edges **[g]**, and apply the frame strips **[h]**. Smooth with a paintbrush and allow to dry completely. Add paste to the back to smooth the seams. File until smooth, adding paste or syringe clay if needed.

TIP

If you don't have access to a rolling mill, texture the copper using dapping tools.

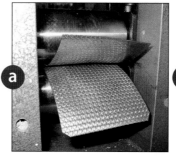
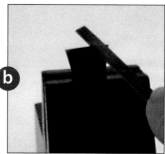
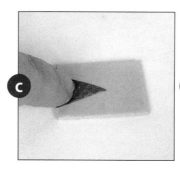
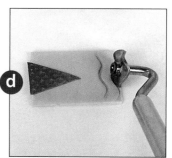
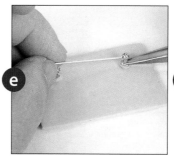
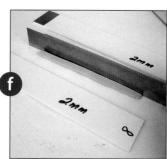

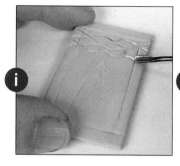

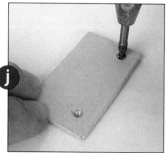

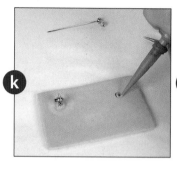

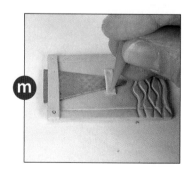

Use a carving tool to enhance the texture on the front, if desired **[i]**.

Pin back assembly

With a drill or a cup bur in a pin vise, enlarge the divots in the back to make shallow holes to hold the pin findings **[j]**. Moisten the holes on the back, apply a coil of syringe clay as if you're creating a bezel, and insert the bolt with the catch attached. Repeat to insert the pin stem and bolt **[k]**.

Smooth the syringe clay around the bolts with a paintbrush **[l]**. Apply extra if needed, smooth, and allow to dry completely. File until smooth.

Roll the excess clay to .75mm thick. Cut a ⅛-in. strip, keeping the edges as smooth as possible to minimize sanding. Place the copper triangle on the top surface of the pin in the prepared space. Trim the strip into a band to fit over the triangle along the frame's left edge. Adhere the band to the dry base by moistening the base and placing paste on the underside of the band where the metal clay pieces meet. Using a green syringe tip, make a small indentation that looks like a rivet in each end of the band. Follow the same steps to create a shorter band across the narrow end of the triangle **[m]**. Allow to dry completely. Sand and smooth the bands if needed.

Remove the pin stem and catch for firing. Fire at 1290°F (700°C) for 15 minutes. Remove from the kiln, allow to cool until just warm, and place into warm pickle to remove the oxidation from the copper. Remove from the pickle and place in a neutralizing solution. Polish with a soft brass brush and soapy water for a matte finish, or tumble polish for a high shine.

Dip the base of the pin stem into a small amount of epoxy, then screw it into the bolt. Repeat for the catch. Allow 24 hours before wearing.

> **TIP**
>
> *Make sure the pin stem and the catch are screwed into the bolts as you make the divots in the wet clay. That way the threaded bolts will not fill with clay. It also helps ensure a good fit. The bolts are made of fine silver and are designed to be fired in place, but you must remove the pin stem and catch for firing.*
>
> **Screw-type pin finding**
>
> catch (do not fire) pin (do not fire)
>
> bolts (fire in place)

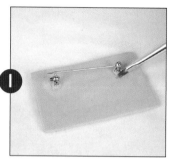

Flowing Rings Pin/Pendant

TECHNIQUES
Metal clay, enameling

The beauty of an Art Deco piece I saw a few years ago stayed with me and inspired the design of this pin. With a hole on one end, the pin is easily converted into a pendant.

MATERIALS

- Art Clay 650 Slow Dry Low Fire: 30g
- Art Clay 650 paste
- Art Clay 650 syringe
- sterling silver wire:
  14-gauge, round, half-hard,
  1 in. (25.5mm)
- three-piece fine silver pin finding
- two-part epoxy
- Thompson 80-mesh enamels:
  #2320 Spring, #2340 Glass,
  #2430 Beryl

TOOLS & EQUIPMENT

- circle cutters and straws ranging
  from 2–14mm
- texturing material (I used a large
  rubber stamp)
- riveting hammer

Metal clay tool kit (p. 87)
Kiln and kiln tools (p. 88)
Finishing tools and supplies (p. 90)
Wireworking tools (p. 91)
Soldering setup (p. 91)
Pickling setup (p. 91)
Enameling tools (p. 93)

PATTERN
Trace or photocopy at 100%

hole for pendant

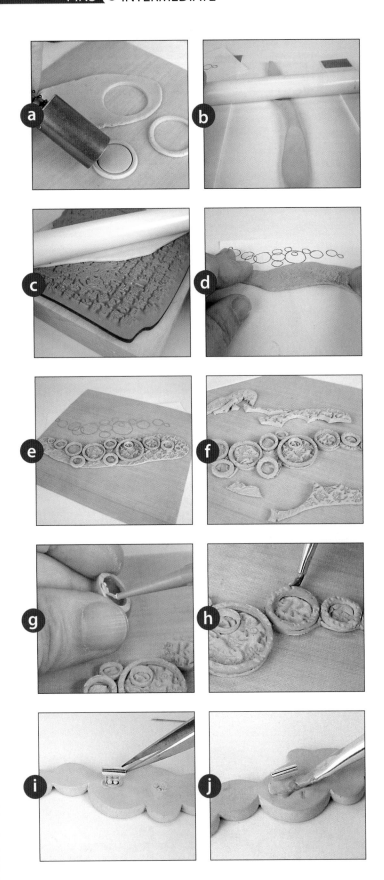

Metal clay rings

Trace or make a photocopy of the pendant pattern. Roll 10g of clay to 3mm thick and texture if desired. Cut a circle in the clay, then use a slightly smaller cutter to cut out the center **[a]**. Use circle cutters with graduated diameters to make rings of metal clay. Cut two 14mm, two 11mm, four 7mm, five 5mm, and one 3mm rings in this way. Dry the rings thoroughly in the dehydrator. When dry, carefully file the inside and outside edges of the rings.

Roll the remaining 20g of clay into a ¼-in. (6mm) diameter snake the length of the rubber stamp. Using 1.5mm spacer slats, roll the snake toward the middle from both ends **[b]**, then side-to-side to widen it. Place the clay on the stamp and roll gently so it doesn't distort or thin too much **[c]**. Use your fingers to shape the clay into a loose S-curve panel the size of the pattern **[d]** and place on a piece of nonstick sheet. Using the template as a guide, position the rings on the panel **[e]**.

Trim the excess clay from the panel **[f]**. Apply syringe clay to the back of each ring and adhere the rings to the panel **[g]**. If desired, make a hole in one end ring for the pendant as shown on the pattern. Dry in the dehydrator.

When completely dry, fill in any gaps, add paste to the seams, and smooth to create a solid frame **[h]**. File and sand smooth. A range of small files will help get into the sharp angles between the circles.

Apply two dots of syringe clay to the back of the panel for the base pieces of the pin finding. Use tweezers to position the catch **[i]** and stem on the back of the panel and smooth with a paintbrush.

Reinforce the points where the catch and hinge attach with thin strips of clay. Roll a pea-sized piece of clay into two .5mm-thick strips about ⅒ x ⅓ in. (2.5 x 8mm) and adhere over the base of the catch and the hinge with paste. Smooth with a paintbrush **[j]**. Using a green syringe tip, press to make a small dimple near the ends of both strips to ensure tight contact and add a decorative touch. Allow to dry, sand, fill any gaps, and finish well.

Prop with fiber blanket for firing. Fire at 1200°F (650°C) for 30 minutes. Remove from the kiln and cool. Use a wire brush and soapy water to shine the piece. Tumble polish.

Enameling the rings

Assemble all your enameling equipment and supplies (see p. 93). Clarify the enamel and use a fine-tip paintbrush to apply the wet enamel to the interior of the rings as desired **[k]**. (I used Spring, a light green, as a base, adding accents of Beryl and Glass.) Add water to the enamel if needed, and tap the edge of the piece to level the enamels. Set the piece on top of the kiln to dry. Check the work for any stray enamel, removing them with the brush.

Place the piece on a trivet, and place the trivet on a kiln shelf. Use a kiln fork to place the shelf into the kiln and fire at 1400°F (760°C) for about two minutes. Remove when the enamel is glossy and set aside to cool. Use an alundum stone under running water to clean any remaining stray enamel from the finished silver. Return to the kiln to flash-fire if needed, then polish with successively finer grits of sanding papers. Polish with a polishing cloth.

Pin back assembly

Next you will reinforce the pin hinge with a rivet made from 14-gauge wire. Using a 1.7mm bit, drill a hole through the indentations in both sides of the hinge. Holding the 14-gauge wire in a pin vise, file or grind one end to a point **[l]**. Ball up the opposite end of the wire with a torch **[m]**. Pickle. Place the pin spring end into the hinge and tighten the assembly with pliers **[n]**. Insert the point of the wire into the hole in one side of the hinge, through the pin spring, and out the other side of the hinge **[o]**. Snug the balled end up to the hinge and snip off about two-thirds of the ball with a wire cutter **[p]** so it has a flat head.

Cut the opposite end of the wire about 1mm past the hinge. With a riveting hammer and a bench block, tap the cut end of the wire until it splays out into a rivet. Hammer both ends of the rivet to flatten the heads **[q]**. File any irregularities smooth and buff with a polishing wheel.

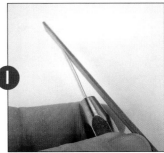

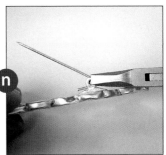
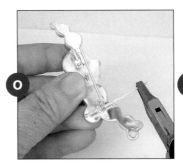
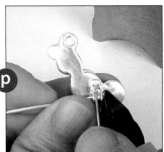
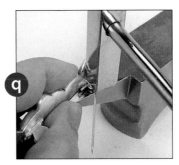
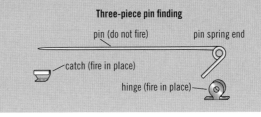

TIP *I used a three-part pin finding for this project. It includes the hinge (to which the pin's spring attaches), the safety catch, and the pin. The hinge and the catch, which are made of fine silver, can be fired in place; the pin must be attached after firing.*

Three-piece pin finding

pin (do not fire)   pin spring end

catch (fire in place)

hinge (fire in place)

Monet Lily Pad Pin

Use syringe and rolled clay to create a free-flowing
design where lilies seem to float in a pond.

MATERIALS

- Art Clay 650 Slow Dry Low Fire: 20g
- Art Clay 650 paste
- Art Clay 650 syringe: green tip,
  blue tip
- sterling silver wire:
  14-gauge, round, half-hard,
  1 in. (25.5mm)
- three-piece fine silver pin finding

TOOLS & EQUIPMENT

- riveting hammer

Metal clay tool kit (p. 87)

Kiln and kiln tools (p. 88)

Finishing tools and supplies (p. 90)

Wireworking tools (p. 91)

Soldering setup (p. 91)

Waves and lily pads

Roll 10g of clay to make two snakes, one about 1.5mm in diameter and the other about 1mm in diameter. Place the snakes together and shape them into a wave as shown **[a]**. Adhere with paste and set aside until completely dry.

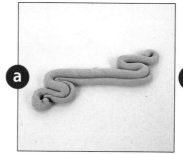
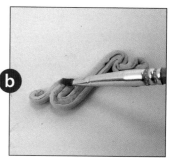

On the back of the wave, add syringe clay and smooth with a brush to create a seamless backing **[b]**. Allow to dry completely and sand smooth.

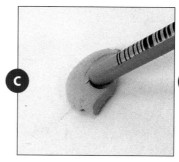

To create the lily pads, roll a dime-sized piece of clay (about 3g) into a ball and flatten it into a disk shape with your finger. Cut the disk in half and use the end of the paintbrush to make a dimple in the clay **[c]**. Add a bit of syringe clay to the dimple **[d]**.

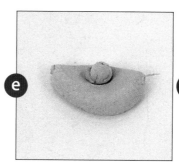

Roll a tiny ball of clay and place it on top of the syringe clay **[e]**. Cut the other half of the disk into slices and attach the ends of each slice to the ball with a brush and paste **[f]**. When the lily pad is firm, use paste to adhere it to the wave. Use a clay shaper to help position the pad **[g]**. Repeat the steps to create and attach a second lily pad. Take care in applying the lily pads to the wave because the pads are fragile.

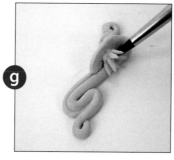
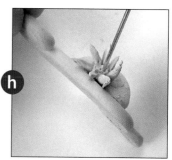

Using a pin or needle tool, make small indentations in the center of each lily to simulate a real flower **[h]**. Prop the pads with a dense, smooth surface (such as a piece of wood) as they dry. Apply syringe clay and paste to gaps and any areas that need reinforcing. Smooth and allow to dry completely. Sand as necessary.

Use about 7g of clay to make another snake 1.5mm in diameter. Shape this second wave as you did the first, making sure it will fit well with the other **[i]**. Do not add paste; first allow to dry completely. Separate the two wave sections and sand any irregularities. Use syringe clay to adhere the two waves together, smooth, and allow to dry. Apply more syringe clay to the back until smooth. Dry, then sand well in preparation for the pin back.

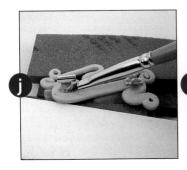

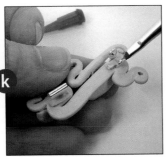

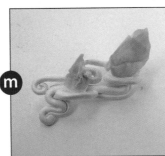

Pin back assembly

Use syringe clay to attach the hinge and catch to the back of the waves as shown. Use foam sanding pads to level the assembly as it dries **[j]**.

Reinforce the points where the head and the catch attach with thin strips of clay. Roll a pea-sized piece of clay into two .5mm-thick strips about 1⁄10 x 1⁄3 in. (2.5 x 8mm) and adhere over the base of the head and the catch with paste. Smooth with a paintbrush **[k]**. Using a blue syringe tip, press to make a small dimple near the ends of both strips **[l]**. This ensures tight contact between the clay pieces and adds a decorative touch. Allow to dry; sand, and fill any gaps. Prop with fiber blanket for firing. Fire at 1290°F (700°C) for 30 minutes. Remove from the kiln and cool. Cover the lily petals with masking tape **[m]** and brush with a wire brush and soapy water. (The lily petals will remain white.)

Next you will add the pin to the hinge, reinforcing the hinge with a rivet as in the Flowing Rings Pin. See p. 63 and follow the pin back assembly steps.

Metal Clay and Ceramic Name Tag

If you have to wear a name tag, why not make it an interesting one? This project combines textured, glazed ceramic clay with metal clay.

TECHNIQUES
Metal clay, beginning ceramics

MATERIALS

- Art Clay 650 Slow Dry Low Fire: 20g
- Art Clay Overlay paste
- Art Clay 650 paste
- Art Clay 650 syringe
- fine silver screw-type pin finding
- 10 sterling silver jump rings: 16-gauge, 3.5mm ID*
- leaves for texturing (I used a fern)
- earthenware clay, white, walnut-sized piece
- low-fire earthenware clay glazes: Moss, Faux Leaves, Blue Patina
- two-part epoxy
- rubbing alcohol or alcohol wipe

TOOLS & EQUIPMENT

- texture wheel
- letter stamps, 1/4 in. (6.5mm)
- teardrop-shaped cutter: 5/8 in. (16mm) (optional)

Metal clay tool kit (p. 87)
Kiln and kiln tools (p. 88)
Finishing tools and supplies (p. 90)
Pickling setup (p. 91)
Ceramics tools (p. 92)

*Add or subtract jump rings based on the number of characters in your name.

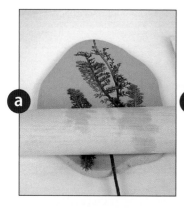

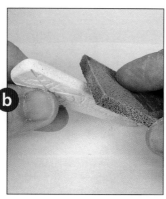

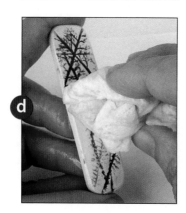

Ceramic panel

Roll the earthenware clay to 4mm thick. Roll the leaves into the clay **[a]** and peel off carefully.

Choose an interesting area of the impression and use a straight-edge cutter to cut a 3 x ⅝ in. (76 x 16mm) panel. If you have a long name, add to the length. Set the panel aside to dry for two to three days, until all the moisture is gone.

Wearing a face mask, sand the edges smooth with a sanding pad **[b]**, curving the corners. Carve into or enhance the design as desired. Dust off the piece.

Use a ball bur to carefully drill two shallow indentations in the back of the piece **[c]** for the threaded bolts that hold the pin stem and catch. For placement purposes, take into account the 12–15% shrinkage that will result from bisque firing, and enlarge the holes with a ball bur or larger drill bit if necessary.

To fire, place in a cold kiln. Bisque fire to 1923°F (1050°C), no hold time, and let the kiln cool naturally.

Glazing the ceramic panel

Apply the first glaze color, Moss, to the leaf veins and wipe off with a very wet paper towel **[d]**. The glaze will remain only in the veins. Let the first glaze dry in the dehydrator before adding more glazes. Glaze the piece with two coats of the Faux Leaves color and one coat of Blue Patina to get the color shown, drying the glazes between coats.

TIP *Overlay paste was designed to work with glass. It adheres well to ceramic glazes. Glaze the back of the tag with at least one coat to ensure good contact with the metal clay and the pin finding.*

Set the piece on two supports on a kiln shelf and glaze fire at 1823°F (995°C) degrees with no hold time. Allow to cool to room temperature before removing from the kiln.

Metal clay panel

Using about 5g of metal clay, roll a snake a little bit longer than the ceramic panel and about ¼ in. (6mm) in diameter. Place the snake against the ceramic panel. Using tweezers, insert half the jump rings about one-third of the way into the clay, spacing them about ¼ in. apart **[e]**. Position the snake so the jump rings point down and run a texture wheel over the length of the jump ring unit **[f]**. Trim the ends to the length of the ceramic panel. Put the assembly in the dehydrator until completely dry. Using syringe clay, fill the indentations made by the jump rings **[g]**. When dry, file and finish.

Apply overlay paste generously across the entire back of the ceramic panel. Run a thick line of overlay paste along the bottom edge of the panel **[h]**. Place some overlay paste along the top of the metal clay unit and adhere to the ceramic panel **[i]**. Let this dry until firm. (Propping the assembly between two sanding pads helps it keep its shape.) On the back, add regular paste or syringe clay to reinforce the join **[j]**. Dry completely. Sand and file the metal clay surfaces.

Use excess clay to roll a snake 2mm in diameter and the length of the name tag. Apply paste to the front seam where the ceramic and metal clay pieces join. Place the snake onto the seam **[k]** and press gently. Use a green syringe tip to add a decorative pattern **[l]**. Dry completely. File, sand, and finish with graduated grits of sanding pads.

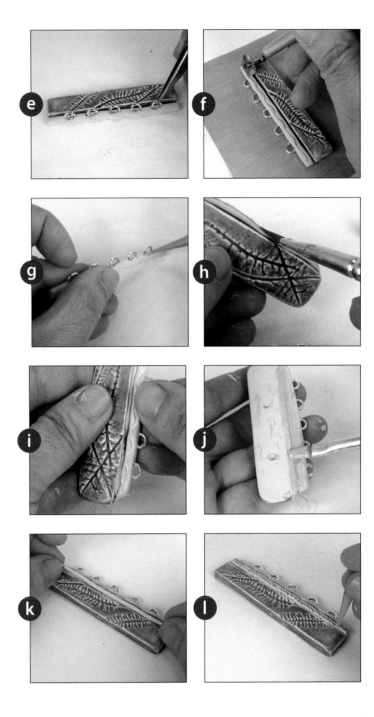

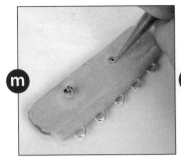

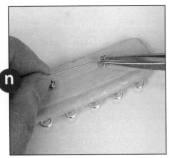

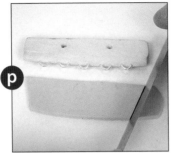

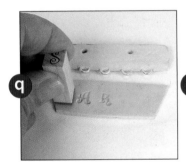

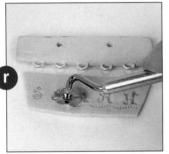

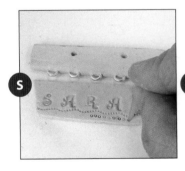

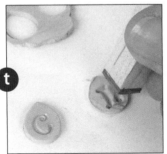

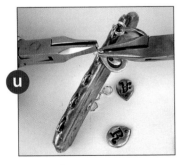

Place syringe clay into one indentation in the back and insert the bolt holding the catch. Add syringe clay to the other indentation **[m]** and insert the bolt holding the pin stem **[n]**. Smooth with a brush. Let dry, propping the pin stem with a foam sanding pad so it doesn't sag **[o]**. Clean the ceramic glaze with rubbing alcohol to remove any metal clay dust.

Remove the pin stem and catch for firing. Ramp up slowly to 1290°F (700°C), hold for 15 minutes, and allow to cool to room temperature. Remove from the kiln and polish with a wire brush and soapy water. Burnish if desired.

Name panel and assembly

Roll out the remaining 15g of metal clay to 2mm thick. Trim to the length of your ceramic panel and about ¾ in. (19mm) wide. Trim the sides at a slant **[p]**. Stamp your name with letters spaced equally across the clay panel **[q]**. Run a texture wheel across the bottom of the panel **[r]**. Use the green syringe tip to make a pattern to match the top panel **[s]**. Set aside to dry completely. Sand and file smooth. Mark and drill holes for the jump rings from which this panel will hang. Fire at 1290°F (700°C) for 15 minutes.

For another name panel option, see the pin on the opening page of this book. To make this version, you'll need a teardrop-shaped cutter a little larger than your alphabet stamps, or you can cut out individual letters by hand. Roll clay to 2mm thick and punch a teardrop shape for each letter in your name. Stamp a letter into each shape **[t]**. Allow to dry completely, sand, and drill a hole in each letter shape. Fire at 1290°F for 15 minutes.

Add a patina to the name panel or individual letters if desired with a liver of sulfur solution. Polish the highlights to a bright shine with metal polish, leaving the letters dark. Using two pairs of pliers, open the jump rings and connect them to the name panel or individual letters and to the name tag **[u]**. Close all the jump rings.

Add a touch of epoxy to the threaded ends of the screw-in pin stem and the catch and screw each element into the bolts. Allow 24 hours before wearing.

Seed Bead Vessel Pin

During a meeting of my artisans group, we challenged each other to make a pot or vessel in our preferred medium. This piece is my result – I hope you enjoy crafting it!

TECHNIQUES
Metal clay, wireworking, beading

MATERIALS

- Art Clay 650 Slow Dry Low Fire: 25g
- Art Clay 650 paste
- Art Clay 650 syringe
- copper wire:
  16- or 18-gauge, round, 6 in. (15.2mm)
- cork clay
- fine silver micro mesh
- fine silver screw-type pin finding
- sterling silver wire:
  28-gauge, round, dead-soft, 3 ft. (9.14m)
- 2g size 15º seed beads, various colors
- two-part epoxy

TOOLS & EQUIPMENT

- scissors for cutting mesh
- texturing material
- **Metal clay tool kit** (p. 87)
- **Kiln and kiln tools** (p. 88)
- **Finishing tools and supplies** (p. 90)

PATTERN
Trace or photocopy at 100%

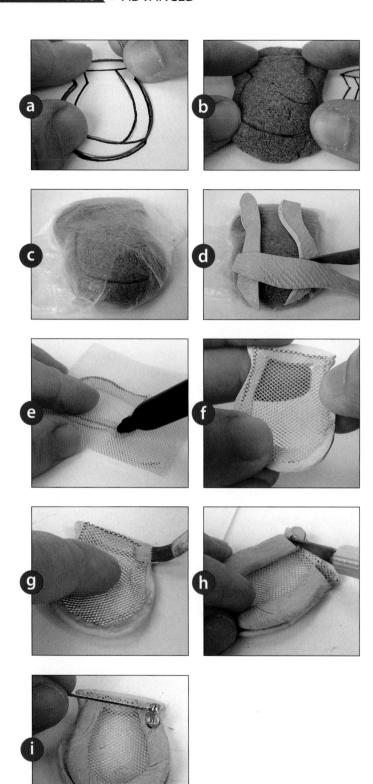

Metal clay vessel

Trace or photocopy the vessel frame pattern. Bend the copper wire to follow the outline of the pattern **[a]**. Shape a piece of cork clay so it is just a bit larger than the pattern, rounding it in the palm of your hand for dimension. Push the wire outline into the clay **[b]**. Trim the cork clay, leaving about ¼ in. (6mm) extra around the wire. Remove the wire and wrap the cork clay armature in plastic wrap **[c]**.

Roll 10g of metal clay to 2mm thick and texture as desired. Using the pattern as a guide, cut strips of clay for the two sides and bottom of the vessel, place over the plastic-wrapped cork clay, and trim **[d]**. Use paste or syringe clay to adhere the frame sides to the bottom piece.

Roll 3g of clay to 2mm thick to make the top strip. Cut, following the pattern, and adhere this strip to the side strips with paste. Dry the assembly over the cork clay armature in the dehydrator until it is completely dry. File and sand until smooth. Apply more paste or syringe clay to any seams and let dry completely.

Place the micro mesh over the back of the vessel assembly. Use a permanent marker to draw the midline of the vessel onto the mesh **[e]**. Cut out the shape with scissors. Gently and carefully mold the mesh to the back of the metal clay frame **[f]**. Paste the mesh in place **[g]** and let dry. Roll the remaining 12g of clay into a ⅛-in. (4mm) diameter snake about 4 in. (10.2cm) long. Flatten to 3mm. Place the flattened snake against the back of the vessel frame in a U-shape and trim the ends **[h]** to form the backing of the vessel. Follow the pattern to cut a strip from excess clay for the top back of the vessel.

Pin back assembly

This four-piece screw-type pin finding is the same as used in the Textured Copper Insert Pin (p. 58). With the pin and the catch screwed tightly into the bolts, push the bolts into the clay **[i]**. This will help to align the pin and the catch. (Don't worry if the pin is too long; you can file it shorter later.) Lift the pin findings out of the clay and remove the U-shaped backing from the mesh. Using a cocktail straw, poke holes all the way through the backing to create seating holes for the bolts **[j]**.

Use a syringe without a tip to apply a thick strip of clay to the back of the vessel **[k]**. Moisten the back of the U-shape and place it on the back of the vessel frame, sandwiching the mesh in the middle. Add the top piece you cut earlier. Fill the outer edges of the vessel frame with syringe or paste and smooth it until the edge appears seamless **[l]**. Paste and smooth the top seam in the same way. Dry the assembly over the plastic-wrapped armature **[m]**. When completely dry, file and sand smooth.

Test-fit the bolts in the holes you made. If necessary, enlarge the holes slightly with a ball bur. Using the green tip, place a layer of syringe clay in the holes **[n]**, then insert the bolts with the pin and catch screwed into place. Prop the pin open with a piece of foam while the syringe clay dries **[o]**. Add syringe clay and paste, drying between applications, until you get a smooth, even finish. Dry, sand, and file.

Unscrew the pin and catch and set them aside. Fire the vessel at 1290°F (700°C) for 30 minutes. Polish with a stainless steel brush to give the vessel a matte finish and use an agate burnisher on the high spots.

> **TIP**
> *Take care when using the 28-gauge wire – as you work, the wire becomes work-hardened, making it stiff and brittle.*

Beaded interior and assembly

Bend the 28-gauge wire in half. You'll insert the wire halfway up the vessel at the edge, where the mesh meets the metal clay. From the back, insert both wire ends into adjacent holes (one above the other) in the mesh. Working with the upper half of the wire first, slip seed beads on the wire **[p]** until they span the width of the vessel **[q]**. Insert the wire at the opposite side, and enter the mesh hole directly above. Repeat this step, moving upward until the top half of the vessel is filled with beads. Tuck the wire end into the mesh to secure. Repeat to fill the vessel's lower half. Screw the pin and catch into the bolts and mark the desired pin length with a permanent marker **[r]**. Cut the pin stem and file it to a point again. Polish the end with a buff and metal polish. Unscrew the pin and catch, add a touch of epoxy for security, then replace the pin and catch. Allow 24 hours before wearing.

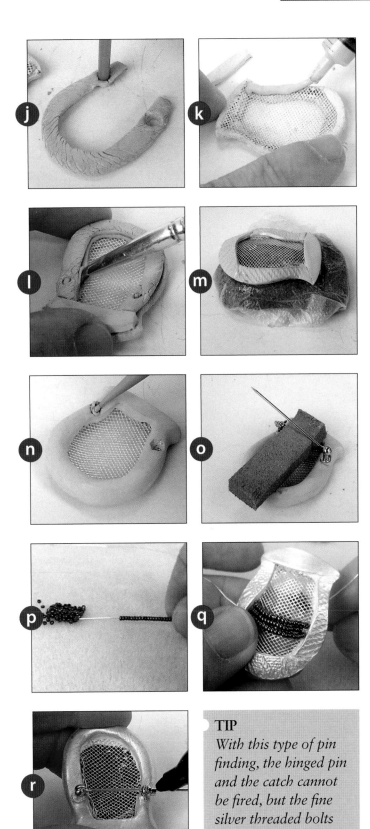

> **TIP**
> *With this type of pin finding, the hinged pin and the catch cannot be fired, but the fine silver threaded bolts that hold these pieces can be fired in place.*

Chapter 5
TOGGLES & CLASPS

I like to finish off my work with a complementary toggle or clasp. Occasionally I use a beautiful toggle as the focal point of the piece. Once you begin creating your own closures for your jewelry designs, you've stepped up to a new level of artistry and craftsmanship.

Lentil-shape Toggle

TECHNIQUE
Metal clay

This lovely, curvaceous toggle drapes well. Change its size to enhance any bracelet or necklace design.

MATERIALS
- Art Clay 650 Slow Dry Low Fire: 15g
- Art Clay 650 paste
- Art Clay 650 syringe
- 2 sterling silver jump rings: 16-gauge, 3.5mm ID

TOOLS & EQUIPMENT
- round cutters:
  1¼ in. (32mm), ⅝ in. (16mm)
- two light bulbs or plastic packaging from light bulbs
- texturing material (I used wallpaper)

Metal clay tool kit (p. 87)

Kiln and kiln tools (p. 88)

Finishing tools and supplies (p. 90)

Pickling setup (p. 91)

TIP *The plastic packaging from small appliance bulbs works well for this project.*

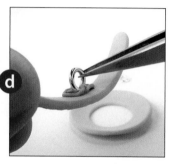

TIP

When I attach jump rings to my toggle bars, I open the ring slightly and place it at a 30-degree angle so the toggle sits neatly on the wrist. If your syringe clay is too soft and the jump ring will not stay put, use props for support until the clay hardens.

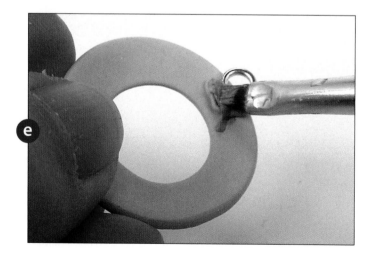

Ring and bar

Roll 10g of clay to 1.5mm thick and texture as desired. Cut a ring using the larger cutter for the outside **[a]** and the smaller cutter for the inside. Remove the inner circle. Drape the disk over the light bulb or packaging. Make a snake from the remaining 5g of clay. Flatten to 1.5mm thick and texture to create the bar. Trim if necessary. Drape the bar over the other light bulb or packaging **[b]**. Set aside to dry.

TIP

The bar of the toggle has to be long enough so that when worn, it doesn't fall out of the toggle hole. For this design, with a ⅝-in. (16mm) hole in the toggle loop, I created a 2-in. (51mm) bar.

When the pieces are firm, remove them from the forms and allow to dry completely. Sand the edges to a smooth finish **[c]**.

Place a bit of moisture and a small mound of syringe clay at the midpoint of the back of the toggle bar. With tweezers, place a jump ring in the mound **[d]** and smooth. Use syringe clay to attach a jump ring to the concave side of the toggle ring and smooth with a brush **[e]**. When dry, add more syringe clay or paste as needed to create a smooth surface.

Fill any holes, gaps, or cracks and let both pieces dry completely. File with progressively finer sandpaper. Angle the toggle slightly while sanding to bevel its edges.

Fire at 1200°F (650°C) for 30 minutes. Remove from the kiln and pickle the pieces. Remove from the pickle and place in a neutralizing bath until it stops bubbling. Brush with a wire brush and soapy water. Tumble polish if desired.

Leaf-and-branch Toggle with Ladybug

This toggle set is a little more elaborate and adds a very refined look to your work. I often use a decorative toggle like this one as a focal piece.

TECHNIQUES
Metal clay, stone setting

MATERIALS

- Art Clay 650 Slow Dry Low Fire: 15g
- Art Clay 650 paste
- Art Clay 650 syringe: green tip, blue tip
- sterling silver jump ring: 16-gauge, 3.5mm ID
- sterling silver wire: 20-gauge, round, half-hard, 2 in. (51mm)
- 3mm garnet cabochon
- two leaves of different sizes (I used rose leaves)

TOOLS & EQUIPMENT

- hole cutters: 3mm, 4mm
- tube light bulb such as a small aquarium bulb

Metal clay tool kit (p. 87)

Kiln and kiln tools (p. 88)

Finishing tools and supplies (p. 90)

Wireworking tools (p. 91)

Pickling setup (p. 91)

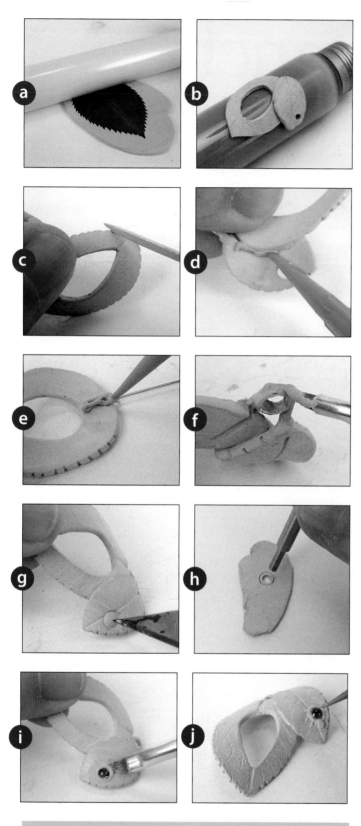

Leaves and ladybug

Roll 10g of clay to 1.5mm thick. Place the larger leaf on the clay and roll to make a good impression **[a]**. Cut the leaf shape out and cut a leaf-shaped hole in the center with a craft knife. Set aside.

Roll 5g of clay to the same thickness. Impress the smaller leaf into it, but do not cut a hole in this one. Using a cocktail straw, poke a hole near the tip of the leaf for the garnet.

Drape the leaves on the bulb with the smaller over the larger **[b]**. Set aside to dry. When the pieces are firm, remove from the bulb and set aside to dry completely.

File shallow grooves in the edges of the leaves **[c]** to simulate a real leaf. Sand the shapes until smooth and well finished. Reinforce the point where the leaves connect with a generous amount of syringe clay **[d]**.

Cut two 1-in. (25.5mm) lengths of wire. Positioning the wire opposite the leaf's point and overlapping about ¼ in. (6mm), attach a wire to each leaf with paste and syringe clay **[e]**. Allow to dry completely. Slide the wire out of the paste enclosure. With roundnose pliers, make a loop in one end of each wire. Reinsert the straight ends of the wires into the leaf shapes, with the loops facing each other. Trim the straight ends of the wires if necessary and adjust the loops so they overlap to form a single circle. Add paste to the exposed wire to adhere the wire loops to each other, creating a solid piece **[f]**. Apply more paste to adhere the wire ends to the leaves.

On the smaller leaf, trim any excess clay from the hole **[g]**. Place the garnet into the hole to check the fit and reshape the hole as necessary so the stone sits straight.

To make a bezel for the garnet, roll a pea-sized bit of clay to .75mm thick and cut a ⅙-in. (4mm) circle with a cocktail straw or brass cutter. Punch out the center of the circle with a smaller cutter **[h]**. Remove the bezel from the excess clay.

Moisten the area around the garnet and place the bezel over the garnet **[i]**. Make sure you have good

TIP

The cutters I used here are very small and precise. They work well for creating tiny holes and bezels such as the one made here (see Resources, p. 94).

contact between the bezel and the leaf. This is the ladybug's body. Let it dry completely. Check the bezel for neatness and sand if necessary. Using a blue-tipped syringe, add the ladybug's legs, head, and antenna **[j]**. Set aside to dry.

Branch bar

Roll excess clay to form a snake 3 in. (76mm) long and ⅛ in. (3mm) in diameter with tapered ends. Cut the snake at a slant, slightly off-center, to create a 1¾ in. (44mm) main branch. Cut two smaller pieces to create shorter branches **[k]**, placing a piece on either side of the main branch **[l]**. Keep the pieces close so they will fit through the hole in the toggle ring. Open a jump ring slightly and press it into the midpoint of the underside of the main branch **[m]**. Remove the jump ring. Add syringe clay and paste the branch parts together. Dry completely. Sand smooth.

Make a syringe mound over the jump ring indentation **[n]**. Place the jump ring in the mound at about a 30-degree angle. Add paste to fill gaps around the jump ring as needed **[o]**. Fill any holes, gaps, or cracks in the bar, allowing to dry between applications. Let dry completely.

Firing and assembly

File all the pieces with progressively finer sandpaper to a smooth finish. Cover the toggle with a piece of fiber blanket and fire at 1200°F (650°C) for 15 minutes. Remove from the kiln and pickle.

Remove the pieces from the pickle, place in a neutralizing bath, and soak until the liquid stops bubbling. Brush with a wire brush and soapy water. Polish in a tumbler or by hand for a high shine, or buff lightly with fine sandpaper for a satin finish. Burnish the high spots. Use care around the garnet so you don't dislodge the stone.

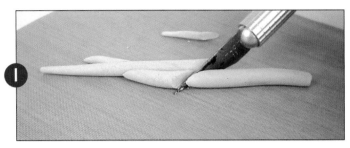

TIP
You can drape the branch at an angle over a light bulb to give it a slight bend or leave it straight.

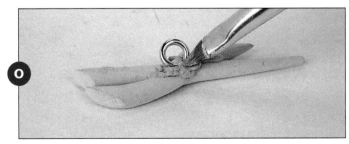

Double-strand Clasp

This attractive clasp uses metal clay for texture and structure and sterling silver for strength. Create it to use in your next double-strand necklace!

TECHNIQUES
Metal clay,
metal
working

MATERIALS

- Art Clay 650 Slow Dry Low Fire: 15g
- Art Clay 650 paste
- Art Clay 650 syringe
- 4 sterling silver jump rings:
  18-gauge, 4mm ID
- sterling silver wire, round,
  half-hard:
  - 14-gauge, 2 in. (51mm)
  - 18-gauge, 2 in.

TOOLS & EQUIPMENT

- rubber stamp for texture
- **Metal clay tool kit** (p. 87)
- **Kiln and kiln tools** (p. 88)
- **Finishing tools and supplies** (p. 90)
- **Wireworking tools** (p. 91)
- **Soldering setup** (p. 91)
- **Pickling setup** (p. 91)

Clasp top

Roll 10g of clay to 1.5mm thick. Texture with a rubber stamp and trim to ⅔ x ⁷⁄₁₆ in. (16 x 11mm) **[a]**. Set aside to dry in the dehydrator. When dry, sand the edges smooth.

With excess clay, roll a snake to 1mm thick and 1½ in. (38mm) long. Align with the long sides of the rectangle and trim to the same length. Apply syringe clay to the two long sides **[b]** and squeeze the snakes up against the rectangle. Smooth any clay that oozes out. Dry completely. Sand the two shorter ends of the rectangle until smooth.

Roll another snake to 1mm in diameter. Trim to fit the short sides of the rectangle, slicing the ends at 45-degree angles **[c]**. Attach with syringe clay as above, and set aside to dry. Sand smooth. Roll another snake longer and slightly thicker than the first to be placed along the underside perimeter. Use a knife to miter the insides of the corners so they join at right angles to form a frame.

Cut a ³⁄₁₆-in. (4.5mm) gap at one end **[d]** and use syringe clay to attach the frame to the underside of the rectangle **[e]**. Smooth the syringe clay on the outside. Apply more syringe clay to the inside and corners. Smooth and set aside to dry completely. Sand the clasp, paying special attention to the cut edges of the opening.

Wire hook

If necessary to allow you to bend it, anneal a 2-in. (51mm) piece of 14-gauge sterling silver wire and pickle it. Use flatnose pliers to bend the wire in half and squeeze it together **[f]**. Place the folded end of the wire on a steel block and hammer the fold flat. Trim to ½ in. (13mm) long. Bend the trimmed ends at about a 45-degree angle to create the hook. (Anneal again if the wire has become work-hardened.)

Turn the clasp over and use a 1.7mm drill bit to drill two shallow indentations near the opening **[g]**. Add syringe clay to the holes, insert the angled end of the hook into the holes, and smooth. Use a small piece of scrap wire to support the hook while you smooth it **[h]** and while it dries.

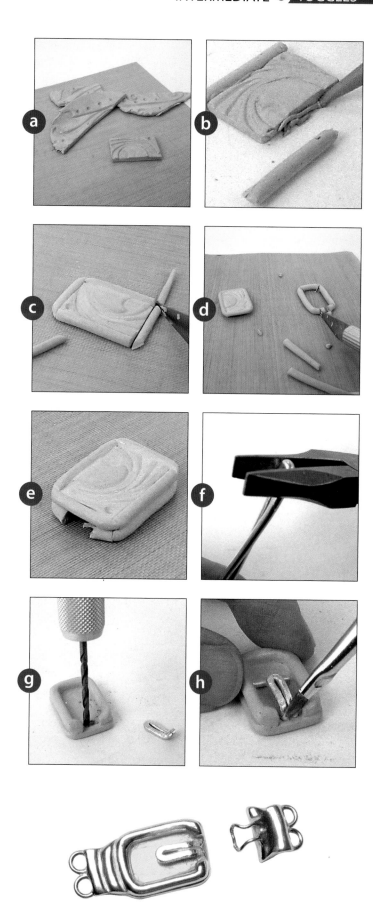

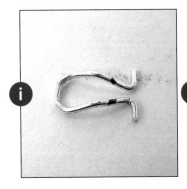

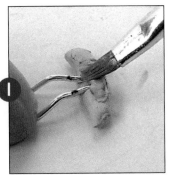

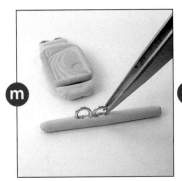

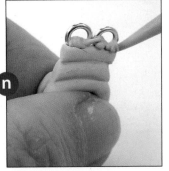

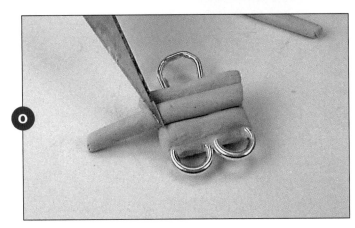

Wire catch and assembly

Use roundnose and chainnose pliers to bend a 2-in. piece of 18-gauge wire for the catch as shown **[i]**. Check the fit of the catch with the hook you made. Adjust the shape of the catch as necessary. File as needed so the hook and catch fit well.

With 2–3g of clay, roll a snake to ⅛ in. (3mm) in diameter. Trim the ends at angles to fit the narrow end of the clasp top and attach it with syringe clay opposite the hook end. Smooth **[j]** and allow to dry. Roll another snake the same diameter. Press the ends of the catch into the snake **[k]**. Check the fit with the clasp and adjust if necessary. Layer syringe clay on top of the ends and smooth **[l]**. Place in the dehydrator to dry. Sand smooth.

Roll a slightly narrower snake and use tweezers to insert two jump rings **[m]**. Use paste to attach the snake to the hook end of the clasp. Trim the ends. Use plenty of syringe clay to secure the jump rings **[n]**. Repeat to make another double jump ring unit for the catch end. Smooth and allow to dry. Fill any gaps, allow to dry again, and sand smooth.

With the remaining 2–3g of clay, roll another narrow snake to apply to both parts of the clasp. Attach this snake with syringe clay between the two original pieces and trim with a craft knife **[o]**. Smooth any excess clay and allow to dry. Sand all parts well with sanding pads and papers. Fire at 1200°F (650°C) for 30 minutes. Cool. Place in warm pickle if you have annealed the wire and caused oxidation. Place in a neutralizing bath. Tumble polish.

Button and T-clasp

This unusual little clasp is about the size of a button. It is small, unobtrusive, and a darling to wear.

TECHNIQUES
Metal clay, wireworking

MATERIALS
- Art Clay 650 Slow Dry Low Fire: 15g
- Art Clay 650 paste
- Art Clay 650 syringe
- 2 sterling silver jump rings:
  16-gauge, 3.5mm ID
- sterling silver wire:
  14-gauge, round, half-hard,
  2 in. (51mm)

TOOLS & EQUIPMENT
- round cutters:
  ⁵⁄₈ in. (16mm), ¾ in. (19mm)
- scrap polymer clay for armature
- small marble for armature
- button for texturing

Metal clay tool kit (p. 87)
Kiln and kiln tools (p. 88)
Finishing tools and supplies (p. 90)
Wireworking tools (p. 91)
Pickling setup (p. 91)

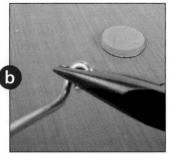

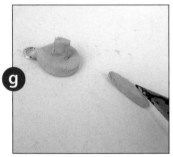

Textured dome

Condition the polymer clay by kneading and set the marble on it as an armature for the domed part of the clasp. Roll 5g of metal clay to 1.5mm thick. Use the ¾-in. (19mm) cutter to cut a disk for the top of the clasp. Impress the button into the metal clay. Form the disk over the marble and allow to dry completely **[a]**. When dry, sand the edge of the disk until smooth. Set aside.

Base and T-stem

Roll 5g of clay to 2.25mm thick (stack the 2mm and .25mm slats to get this thickness). Cut a disk with the ⅝-in. (16mm) cutter for the base. With roundnose pliers, form a small loop at one end of the wire. Position your chainnose pliers over the loop **[b]** and bend the wire at a 90-degree angle so the loop acts like a small foot. Trim the straight end of the wire to a bit longer than ⅛ in. (4–5mm).

Place the foot in the ⅝-in. base so the wire end protrudes from the center. Make a good impression, but don't push the foot all the way through. Attach the foot to the base with syringe clay, smoothing and adding more clay as needed **[c]**. The base should be as smooth and flat as possible so the domed top sits correctly when worn. Use syringe clay to attach a slightly open jump ring to the edge of the disk **[d]** and smooth with a brush. Add paste or syringe clay as necessary for a smooth finish, allowing to dry between applications.

Roll excess clay to 4mm thick and cut a piece to a generous 3/16 in. (5mm) square. Cut through the center about halfway down, so the clay looks like a book **[e]**. Wrap the clay around the wire post. Add paste to close the seam. Add paste and syringe clay around the base of the stem and smooth with a brush **[f]**. Roll excess clay to 2mm thick and ½ in. (13mm) long and taper its ends **[g]**. Paste on top of the stem, curving the ends downward. You will further refine the T-shape after it dries. Make sure the top of the T is no wider than its base.

Add paste or syringe clay to any holes or gaps. Smooth with a brush **[h]** and set aside to dry.

TIP
The T-stem keeps the clasp closed, so the top needs a curve that matches the curve of the dome.

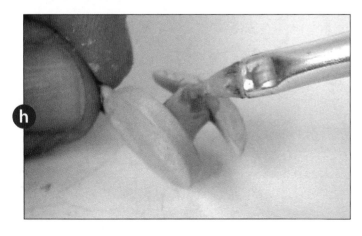

Clasp side wall and bottom

Roll 5g of clay to 1.5mm thick. Punch a disk with the ¾-in. cutter. Using a craft knife or pin tool, cut a rectangle in the center of the disk **[i]** and remove. Notch one long side of the rectangular hole. Set aside to dry. When the disk is firm, add a jump ring to the edge nearest the notch **[j]**

The base may need some fine-tuning to get the top of the T to fit well. File and scrape any extra clay from the inside of the rectangle so that the T fits into it smoothly and you can turn the pieces so the jump rings are opposite each other.

For the side wall, roll a snake to 2mm in diameter and 2 in. (51mm) long. Flatten to 1.5mm thick and trim the width to a little less than ¼ in. (6mm). Add syringe clay around the perimeter of the base and attach the side wall **[k]**. Place the seam next to the jump ring. Fill any gaps with syringe clay or paste and allow to dry completely.

Adjust the height of the side wall by sanding **[l]** so that when the top is attached, it sits nicely. Do not remove too much from the wall – keep checking the height as you sand to ensure the correct fit **[m]**. You may also have to sand the outside of the walls to get a nice contour and a flush fit with the top **[n]**. Place syringe clay along the top of the side wall **[o]** and position the domed cap. Smooth out any excess and add paste or syringe clay as necessary to create a seamless piece **[p]**. Sand to a fine finish.

Fire at 1290°F (700°C) for 30 minutes. Remove from the kiln and cool. Pickle, then soak in a neutralizing bath to remove excess pickle. Polish with a wire brush and soapy water. Tumble polish.

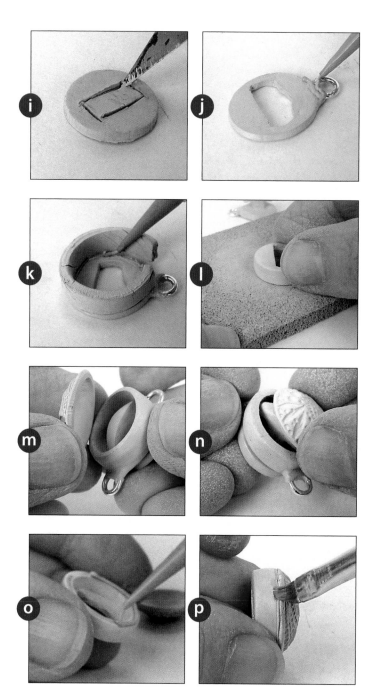

Basics

Many of the tools listed in this section will be used frequently as you work through the projects. For ease of reference and to keep the project supply lists shorter, I have compiled lists of essential tools and supplies here. Please refer to these lists and assemble the tools before you begin to work. Read the entire project to familiarize yourself with the steps before beginning, since you won't need every item from a tool kit for every project.

Types of metal clay

The projects in this book call for Art Clay products – Art Clay 650 Low Fire clay, paste, and syringe forms. Both brands of clay that are currently on the market, Art Clay and PMC, have similar qualities and can be used successfully to create the projects. If you use PMC, take into consideration differing firing schedules and shrinkage factors.

Metal clay in lump form is the base for all the projects in this book. Other types include syringe clay, oil paste (used for repairs), overlay paste (for ceramics and glass), and paper or sheet (handy for origami, decorations, and punched or cut shapes).

Syringe clay is used to fill cracks and create designs. Use syringe clay to extend a tapered snake to create forms such as branches. I find it easiest to hold the syringe in my dominant hand with my thumb pressing the plunger, supporting my arm with the other hand. Experiment to find the way that works best and is most comfortable for you.

Art Clay offers three tips to use with its syringe for extruding the clay to different thicknesses: small (blue tip), medium (green tip), and large (gray tip). I use the green tip most often, but the others are handy for other tasks. To keep the syringes hydrated when you're not using them, store them with the tips in water.

Paste clay is usually applied with a fine-tip paintbrush. Use paste to coat a leaf or other organic or delicate items you want to preserve in silver. You can also trowel it on with a palette knife to create more earthy textures or to build up a low spot in your design.

Overlay paste is specially formulated to work with glass, ceramics, and pottery. It has a different consistency than regular paste and can be used with ceramic pieces to create some very interesting and beautiful jewelry. In a pinch, it also can be thinned with water and used in place of regular paste.

Oil paste is another paste form that is very useful in making repairs (see p. 89).

Paper or sheet clay is a versatile product that can be folded, cut, applied to many surfaces, and used as an addition to enameling and glass fusing. Although the projects in this book do not call for this type of clay, you may enjoy experimenting with paper clay.

Metal clay basic techniques

Since metal clay begins to dry out the moment you open its packaging, it's always a good idea to have all your tools at hand so you are ready to begin shaping the clay immediately. Here are a few tips for keeping clay humidified and workable:
- Always use a moisture barrier on your hands and on tools that come into contact with the clay. A very light application is all you need – try olive oil or Badger Balm.
- Place plastic wrap or a moistened paper towel over the clay, and put excess clay back in its packaging or in a clay keeper.
- Spray a fine mist of water on the clay from time to time.
- Run a small humidifier near your work area.
- Add a tiny drop of glycerin to the clay.

Nearly every jewelry-making project you do will start with rolling the lump of metal clay to flatten it. In the projects in this book, I give the target thickness in millimeters. I use color-coded spacer slats to measure this dimension, but some people use stacked playing cards as their reference. This chart gives you equivalents for comparison.

METAL CLAY THICKNESS GUIDE

Measurement	Slat color	Playing card(s)
.25mm	black	1
.5mm	yellow	2
.75mm	green	3
1mm	blue	4
1.5mm	red	6
2mm	purple	8

Learning to roll a snake of clay to a consistent diameter is a very handy skill. You'll need a different kind of roller for this – a piece of clear acrylic. Some have a handle or ball attached for ease of use, or you can add one yourself with epoxy. Because you can see through the acrylic, you can easily judge the diameter and length of the snake as you roll the clay.

My clear sheet is long, 4 x 10 in. (10.2 x 25.4cm), with a handle made from a wood sphere. I sanded the wood and the sheet and joined them with epoxy. Use a side-to-side motion as you roll.

Metal clay tool kit

These are the basic tools you should have ready as you start the metal clay portion of any project. I've included notes about some of the tools to help those who are new to metal clay.

- **roller** – a short segment of ⅞-in. (22mm) diameter PVC pipe
- **spacer slats** or playing cards to gauge the thickness of rolled clay; see the equivalency chart on p. 86
- **straight-edge clay blade** – sometimes called a tissue blade; a clay scraper also works
- **cleanup tool** – this tool has a double-edged, pointed blade on one end and a pointed scoop on the other
- **snake roller** – a piece of clear acrylic (see above)
- **fine-tip paintbrushes** in three sizes – #4 and #6 chisel blenders, and a #10/0 shader
- **small cup of water** to moisten paintbrushes
- **clay shaper** – also called a wipeout tool; has rubber tips
- **pin tool** or awl
- **hand drill** – with various sizes of drill bits (my set runs from 1.05mm up to 2mm; I use 1.7mm most often because it makes perfectly sized holes for 16-gauge jump rings)
- **tweezers**
- **clay keeper or plastic wrap** to keep clay moist
- **small mister bottle** with water
- **olive oil and sponge** in small container (such as a film canister) or other nonstick balm or spray
- **clay cutters** – I use Kemper Klay Kutters and aspic cutters
- **precision circle cutters** – set of small-diameter hole punches
- **ruler** showing metric and inches
- **straws** – drinking and cocktail straws (cut to short lengths)

Tool kit continued on p. 88

Metal clay tool kit (continued)

- **work surface** – can be a smooth tile, a plastic report cover, or a nonstick cutting mat (anything that clay won't stick to)
- **nonstick Teflon sheets** for drying your work and for wrapping around mandrels
- **3M foam sanding pads** in three grits: medium, fine, and superfine (can be found in paint department)
- **3M Tri-M-Ite sanding papers** in seven color-coded grits: 400, 600, 1200, 2000, 4000, 6000, and 8000; can be used wet or dry
- **drying station** – food dehydrator used only for metal clay
- **two-part molding compound** or polymer clay
- **texturing tools** – my favorites include embossed wallpaper; rubber stamps; brass and rubber texture plates; sewing notions (elastic, ribbon, and fabric); texture rolling tools
- **cup for keeping syringe tubes hydrated** – I use Linda's Lids
- **toothpicks/wood skewers**
- **carving tools**

You may find that you collect more and more tools as you continue your adventure in metal clay. Don't worry – this seems to be a normal part of working with this medium!

Kiln and kiln tools

A kiln is a versatile piece of equipment. You can use it to fire metal clay as well as enamel, ceramics, and glass. Lampworkers use kilns to anneal, which strengthens glass beads by heating them to a certain temperature and then slowly cooling them.

The projects in this book are presented with instructions for kiln-firing in a programmable electric kiln. In my studio, I use a Paragon SC-2, a large, programmable kiln that is well suited for firing metal clay work. There are many kiln manufacturers and many styles of kilns, ranging from small, portable units to large, temperature-regulated models like the SC-2. I suggest you research and learn all you can about kilns to find a model that fits your needs and budget before you invest in this wonderful piece of equipment.

Your kiln will come with instructions. Please take time to learn how it operates before you use it. Because working with a programmable kiln involves super-high heat, you need certain tools to get things done safely. Refer to this list and assemble your kiln needs before firing:

- **programmable electric kiln**
- **kiln fork**
- **long tweezers**
- **kiln furniture** (shelves, posts to raise the shelf off the kiln floor, fiber blanket)
- **fireproof surface(s)** for kiln and staging area
- **safety glasses** with Aura 99 lens

TIP *When looking into and working around an open kiln, you need safety glasses to prevent damage to your eyes. The most common lenses for metal clay kiln work are the Aura 99, #2.0 IR. Using safety glasses every time you open your kiln door protects your eyes from UV and IR radiation and provides a physical barrier from heat and debris.*

If you don't have the room for or aren't ready to invest in a full-sized kiln, you have several options for firing small metal clay pieces (no larger than about 1 in. [25.5mm] in diameter). One option is to use a small butane torch. Another option is to fire small pieces on a gas stovetop, using a wire grid to hold the pieces. Other good alternatives to a full-sized kiln are the SpeedFire Cone system, which is fueled by propane gas, and the small, portable UltraLite electric kiln. No matter how you fire your metal clay, make sure you follow the manufacturer's instructions and safety guidelines. Serious injury can occur with any these methods of firing if you're not careful.

A repair

TECHNIQUE
Repairing cracks

Here is a step-by-step account of an actual repair I made. After I fired the Flowing Rings Pin, two cracks appeared. This repair project details how I restored the piece.

MATERIALS & TOOLS
● Art Clay Oil Paste, 650 Slow Dry Low Fire
● Art Clay Overlay Paste
● sandpaper
● palette knife or flexible spatula
● craft knife or scalpel
● clay shaper
● sanding pads, 400–1200 grit
● roller
● .75 spacer slats
● dehydrator

In my experience with metal clay, "things happen." Perhaps a piece is broken or it needs a new design element. Sometimes a piece comes out of the kiln cracked or the elements just fall completely apart. These unexpected developments can be downright discouraging to the new or not-so-new metal clay artist.

Repair is an essential skill that is learned by experience. All repairs are not the same, and, I'm sorry to say, there is no blanket solution. The good news is that metal clay is very forgiving, and a skillful repair will be hardly noticeable – if it shows at all.

Art Clay Oil Paste is my product of choice for metal clay repairs. Oil paste can be used on pieces made from either Art Clay or Precious Metal Clay (PMC) to repair fired silver and to add parts to fired silver. Follow the manufacturer's instructions to mix and store oil paste.

When repairing a crack or broken piece or adding another element to your design, apply the oil paste with a toothpick, brush, or palette knife. Oil paste gets down into the small cracks and fissures of the broken work to ensure proper adhesion. If you clean up as much oil paste as possible from the piece before firing, you will not have to do as much filing or sanding after firing.

Apply paste and let the repair dry at least 24 hours before firing. Because of its unique formula, oil paste takes longer to air dry than regular and overlay paste.

Small cracks appeared between the rings in this pin after it was fired **[a]**. To begin the repair, I roughed up the repair areas with sandpaper. I applied a thick coat of oil paste with a palette knife, using pressure to push the paste deep into the cracks **[b]**.

Next I applied oil paste to cracks on the sides **[c]**. I used a craft knife to scrape off excess paste **[d],** which I returned to the jar. I dried the piece overnight.

The next day, I added overlay paste to the damaged areas I covered earlier. I rolled a bit of clay to .75mm, cut small strips, and patched the repairs. I used a clay shaper to blend the edges while the clay was soft **[e]**.

I dried the piece in the dehydrator, then sanded lightly with graduated grits of sanding pads for a smooth finish. I refired at 1472°F (800°C) for 30 minutes, removed the piece from the kiln, cooled it, and polished it by hand **[f]**.

If your repaired area is not totally smooth, file or sand it with various grits of files, sanding pads, or sandpaper.

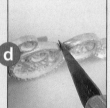
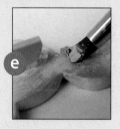
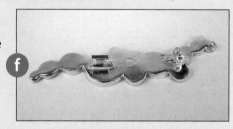

Finishing tools and supplies

The tools required for tumbling and polishing vary, depending on the type of finish you hope to achieve. Here are a few of the basics you'll need for the projects in this book:

• **agate burnisher**
• **wire brush** – brass or stainless steel
• **rotary tool**
• **3M radial polishing disks** – ¾ in. (19mm); sizes 36X to P400X and 1-micron light green (used with rotary tool)
• **other attachments for rotary tool** – ball bur, grinding stone, buff, stone-setting burs, cup burs
• **mechanical rotary tumbler** with stainless steel shot and burnishing compound
• **metal polish**
• **liver of sulfur**

The first step in polishing a piece after it is fired is to use a brass brush under running water with soap for a soft, brushed finish. To keep your brush in good shape, brush only in one direction with gentle strokes – do not scrub the piece harshly. A stainless steel brush used the same way will produce more of a matte, lightly textured finish. Both brushed finishes look good with the high spots burnished with an agate burnisher. You can use a rotary tool with 3M polishing disks to get a nice finish too. Another method is to use metal polish with a buffing wheel on the rotary tool, or use metal polish, a soft cloth, and lots of elbow grease.

To polish the tiny nooks of a piece, I use the tip of an agate burnisher, or you can use a thrumming string, an old-fashioned alternative. This is simply cotton string (like packaging string) that you have coaxed apart into just one or two threads. Place polishing compound on it, tie it to your bench or vise, hold the other end tightly, and polish away! Wash pieces with soapy water after polishing to remove the compound.

Another way to bring up the shine on your metal clay pieces is to tumble them for several hours or overnight in a mechanical rotary tumbler loaded with stainless steel mixed shot, burnishing compound, and water. An advantage of the rotary tumbler is that it work-hardens a piece in the same way that hammering does, making it more durable. Vibrating and magnetic tumblers work well for polishing but are more costly than rotary tumblers.

Wireworking tools

You don't need many tools for the wireworking portion of the projects, and most of these are hand tools:

- **flush cutters**
- **pliers** – flatnose, roundnose, long chainnose
- **cup burs** – I roll between my index finger and thumb to finish the ends of ear wires; you also can use a rotary tool
- **wood dowels** – ¼ in. (6mm), 7⁄16 in. (11mm)
- **sandpaper** – in a wide range of grits up to 2000
- **hand drill and set of drill bits** and rubber block
- **hammers** – planishing, riveting
- **bench block** or small anvil
- **file set** – small, good quality for fine work; a good range would include flat, square, round, and half-round 4s
- **jeweler's saw** or shears
- **pin vise**
- **bracelet step mandrel** or soft-drink can
- **rawhide mallet**

Soldering setup

I use either a MAPP gas torch or an oxy-acetelyne torch. For the projects in this book, a small butane torch would do the job as well. If you're interested in getting a more powerful torch setup, research your options and follow all safety precautions and manufacturer's instructions. Here's what you'll need for the projects in this book:

- **soldering torch** – oxy-propane, MAPP gas, oxy-acetelyne
- **solder** – pallions or wire (hard)
- **soldering flux** (paste)
- **charcoal block** or other heat-proof block
- **titanium solder pick**
- **third hand** tweezers and base

Pickling setup

- **pickle solution**
- **Pyrex cups**
- **copper tongs**
- **neutralizing bath**

After soldering any sterling silver pieces such as wire or jump rings, you'll need to pickle the piece to remove oxidation. I like to use a nontoxic pickle solution such as Silver Prep or Citrex. My pickling station is simple: It consists of a Pyrex measuring cup for hot water and the pickle solution. A small electric crock that you use only for pickling works well too. When the piece turns white in the pickle, place it in a neutralizing bath – a cup of hot water mixed with 1 tablespoon of baking soda – until the piece stops bubbling.

Ceramics tools and techniques

You'll need a very basic ceramic tool setup for the earrings project on p. 17 and for the name tag pin on p. 67:

- **wood dowel** – ¾ in. (19mm) diameter
- **small piece of cotton fabric**
- **2mm spacer slats** or items of same thickness
- **saucer of water**
- **ceramic slip**
- **3M sanding pads** dedicated to ceramics (designed for painting, in medium, fine, and superfine grits)
- **straight-edge blade**

The projects in this book call for low-fire earthenware clay, firing it to bisque, glaze firing, and then adding the metal clay elements to the ceramic pieces.

To condition earthenware clay, you knead it just like bread dough. Press the heel of your hand into the clay and push away several times, then beat it with the wood dowel before rolling it out. Working with this type of clay gets all your aggression out!

Small work in earthenware clay usually takes about 3–7 days to dry, depending on your climate. You can use the dehydrator used for metal clay to speed the drying process. To test for dryness, put the earthenware piece in an airtight plastic storage bag. If the piece is not dry, moisture will appear in the bag. Thorough drying is very important because, just as with metal clay, residual moisture can cause the piece to crack or break as it fires in the kiln.

When your earthenware piece is completely dry, it's time to bisque fire. Bisque firing is the process of baking the moisture out of the clay and hardening it for glaze firing. Low-fire earthenware clay should be bisque fired at 1923˚F (1050˚C) with no hold time. Place the piece in a cold kiln. Ramp up slowly; set the kiln to ramp up to 1923˚F (or cone 05), at either slow speed or 600˚F (315˚C) per hour. It may take as long as 3 hours to reach temperature; let the piece cool naturally. Allow approximately 6 hours or longer total firing and cooling time, depending on how your kiln holds heat. A smaller kiln will cool relatively quickly.

After bisque firing, it's time to glaze. Use three coats of glaze if you are using a paintbrush (recommended for the projects in this book), or you can dip the work in a large bowl of glaze. Let the glaze dry completely overnight. Place the piece in a cold kiln. Glaze fire to 1823˚F (995˚C) (cone 06), no hold time, and let the kiln cool naturally. After firing, the piece is ready for its silver elements.

Enameling tools

The projects in this book that include enameling are a most-basic introduction to the wonderful art of enameling. They call for specialized supplies and equipment:

- **enamel powders** – 80 mesh for the projects in this book
- **fine-tip paintbrushes**
- **enamel spatula** (like a tiny spoon)
- **plastic teaspoons**
- **distilled water**
- **white paper** for work surface
- **bright task light**
- **two plastic cups** filled with water
- **eyedropper** or pipette
- **trivets**
- **mica sheets**
- **particle-safe face mask**
- **Klyr-Fire enamel adhesive**
- **magnifier** on a stand or visor
- **masking tape** and/or permanent marker for marking enamel numbers on spoons
- **glass brush**
- **ammonia** – ammonia wipes are handy
- **face mask** – N95 or N100
- **alundum stone** – used to grind off unwanted enamel
- **sanding pads** in medium, fine, and superfine
- **flatnose pliers**
- **long chainnose pliers**

If you are serious about enameling, I encourage you to learn as much as you can about this ancient art form from the many great resources available. On your way, enjoy, explore, and experiment!

PLEASE USE CAUTION!

Enamels are pieces of glass ground into powdery granules. They are available in leaded or lead-free formulations. Because the use of enamels includes the risk of inhaling or ingesting the glass particles, use a particulate face mask or respirator whenever you're handling enamels, including while sifting or screening. Your work area and clothing should be washed and cleaned thoroughly when you are finished enameling to minimize the spread of the finely ground glass. See p. 94 for more about enameling techniques.

Enameling techniques

Enamels fuse around 1400°F+ (760°C). Preheat the kiln to 1560°F (850°C) or so before you begin. The kiln loses heat when the door is opened, so you have to compensate for the heat loss. Set up your enameling station while the kiln preheats. Place a piece of tape on the handle of each spoon and label the enamel color number.

To clarify enamel: Wearing a face mask, place a scoop or two of enamel into a plastic teaspoon. Close the enamel jar. Using a pipette, carefully add a few drops of clean water to the enamel in the spoon. Gently agitate to separate the "fines" from the heavier enamel. Pour the water containing the fines into a waste cup. Repeat until the water in the spoon is clear (or close to it). Add a drop or two of Klyr-Fire to the spoon and your enamel is ready to use.

What to do with the waste cup of "fines"? I pour the waste water into a coffee filter and leave the fines in the cup to dry. Place the dried enamel into a covered jar to use for counter-enameling.

Applying enamel: Before you apply enamel, I recommend that you tumble polish your metal clay for at least four hours or burnish by hand. Because metal clay is porous even after firing, it has a tendency to absorb water as you apply enamel. You may find you need to add even more water. "Charging" the enamels this way makes it easier to level them.

Firing: Dry the piece on top of the kiln. When enamel is dry, it looks like powder. Place the piece on a trivet, place the trivet on a small metal grid, put your kiln glasses on, and open the kiln. Use a kiln fork to move the trivet/grid assembly into the kiln. Quickly close the door and wait until the temperature returns to 1400°. Wait 1½–2 minutes and check the enamel. You are looking for a glossy finish. If the enamel still looks grainy, wait until the kiln reaches fusing temperature again and refire the piece for another minute or two. Remove the enameling assembly from the kiln to cool naturally.

Sometimes the enamel does not come out perfectly. If there are gaps, or it just needs a little more color, apply more enamel, level it out, let it dry, and re-fire.

You can stone off stray enamel with an alundum stone under running water. After cleaning the piece with a glass brush, flash-fire the piece if necessary. Set the kiln to 1560°; fire the piece for 45 seconds to 1 minute until it returns to the glossy state. Don't overfire; delicate colors can burn. Cool.

Resources

Lapidary
Custom gem cutting
Mark White
(603) 493-4856
fusionstatements.com

Art Clay, tools, kilns, and firing supplies

Art Clay World USA
(866) 381-0100
artclayworld.com

Whole Lotta Whimsy
(520) 531-1966
wholelottawhimsy.com

The Contenti Company
(401) 421-4040
contenti.com

Art Clay Supply
(800) 388-2001
artclaysupply.com

Ceramic clay, kilns, and firing supplies

Amaco
(800) 374-1600
amaco.com

Clay-King
(888) 838-3625
clay-king.com

Out on a Limb Studio
Earthenware clay in small amounts
(603) 882-8180

Enamels

Enamelwork Supply
(800) 596-3257

Schlaifer's Enameling Supply
(800) 525-5959
enameling.com

Thompson Enamel
(859) 291-3800
thompsonenamel.com

Tools, supplies

Santa Fe Jewelers Supply
Precious metals and wire, jewelers tools
(800) 659-3835
sfjssantafe.com

Cool Tools
Specialty tools, nontoxic silver pickle
(888) 478-5060
cooltools.us

Creative Texture Tools
Precision Circle Cutters, silicone texture mats, tools
(708) 488-9589
creativetexturetools.com

Whole Lotta Whimsy
Glazes, tools, kilns, kiln tools
(520) 531-1966
wholelottawhimsy.com

PMC Supply
Rubber stamp mats are the best!
(800) 388-2001
pmcsupply.com

Silver and Spice Jewelry
Sterling silver and gold-filled jump rings, all diameters
silverandspicejewelry.com

Books

Art Clay Silver & Gold Metal Clay: The Complete Guide
by Jackie Truty

Creative Metal Clay Jewelry
by CeCe Wire

Enameling on Metal Clay
by Pam East

The Art of Enameling
by Linda Darty

Keum-Boo on Silver
by Celie Fago

The Complete Metalsmith
by Tim McCreight

Tumble Finishing for Handmade Jewelry
by Judy Hoch

Internet reading

Margaret Shindel's Squidoo lens site contains a wealth of information on all aspects of metal clay.

Types of metal clay
squidoo.com/metal-clay-types

Tools and supplies
squidoo.com/metal-clay-tools

Instructional videos

Cool Tools
cooltools.us
Free online instructional videos for metal work and metal clay

About the author

Carol A. Babineau was born and raised in New England. Drawing, watercolor painting, sewing, and quilt making are some of the many ways Carol enjoys expressing herself and her artistic vision. She loves and learns from nature, reveling in the beautiful northeastern countryside that surrounds her.

Carol is an Aida Certified Art Clay Senior Instructor, a State Juried Member of the League of New Hampshire Craftsmen, a juried member of the Dunstable Artisans, a member of the Enamel Guild North East, and a PMC Connection Certified Artisan (Levels I & II).

Carol continues to share her excitement for metal clay through publishing and teaching. She has published articles in *Art Jewelry* and *Bead&Button* magazines, and she teaches from her studio in the Picker Building, Nashua, N.H.

Author photos by Ella Putney Carlson | ellaprints.com

Dedication

This book is dedicated to Sharon Hill, without whom I would have never taken that first class. I'd also like to thank my husband, Norm, and all my family and closest friends – without their support the book would still be just an idea. Thanks also to my daughter, Sarah J. Babineau, a goldsmith by trade – she is always there for whatever I need. She is a great asset and assists me with her thoughts on design kinks and her skills at the bench.

To Carla Eaton, for positive vibes and support along the way. She gave me a space within River Art Studios where my metal clay adventure blossomed and grew.

To Michela Verani, an exceptional artist, who has freely given me her help and friendship. She always listened and understood my ideas and supported my vision.

To Tonya Davidson for her great technical assistance.

To Mark White for his support and exceptional cut gems.

To my publishing friends at Kalmbach.

To all the people I have met along the way, my friends at the Picker Building, my students, and all those who knew I could do it!

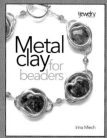

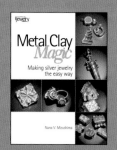
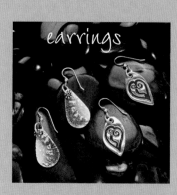